Assessment Program

Grade 4

ISBN 0-15-310205-5

1 2 3 4 5 6 7 8 9 10 073 2000 99 98 97

Harcourt Brace & Company

Orlando   Atlanta   Austin   Boston   San Francisco   Chicago   Dallas   New York   Toronto   London

http://www.hbschool.com

Assessment Program

Assessment is an ongoing process that is integral to helping students increase their understanding and appreciation of artworks and art processes. Meaningful and appropriate assessment improves both the content and outcomes of art instruction. It provides the information needed to make sound decisions regarding the art curriculum and how to implement it effectively.

The *Art Express Assessment Program* makes it easy for teachers to formally and informally evaluate students' understanding of the content in each lesson in the *Pupil Edition*.

- Two reproducible assessment pages are provided that correspond to each lesson in the *Pupil Edition*, beginning with an objective set of items to assess vocabulary and concept knowledge. Each lesson-level assessment also includes a writing prompt like those found in state writing assessments. The writing prompt requires students to use what they have learned to write a composition such as an informative essay, a persuasive letter, or a story. A detailed, prompt-specific graphic organizer leads students through the writing task, guiding them to include the important aspects of the particular writing form.

- A two-page review at the end of each unit provides additional opportunities to assess student learning. Review activities—presented in a variety of assessment formats, including popular standardized test formats—assess students' knowledge of unit vocabulary and concepts as they relate to the unit theme.

- Rubrics are provided to help evaluate student compositions. As an alternative, teachers may choose to have students assess and reflect on their own work using the self-evaluation checklists also provided.

- Additional evaluation instruments that can be used to informally assess student artworks, portfolios, interests, and essential knowledge are provided as blackline masters.

- The Word Card blackline masters can be duplicated and used to help students learn and review important art vocabulary.

Whether you prefer formal or informal evaluation, the *Art Express Assessment Program* provides ongoing and regular opportunities to reflect on students' progress and make informed instructional decisions.

Contents

Harcourt Brace School Publishers

Harcourt Brace School Publishers

Name _____

Vocabulary and Concepts

> petroglyphs
> outline
> carved

A Complete each sentence with a word from the box.

1. Long ago, artists _____ lines in rock walls with sharp objects.

2. Pictures scratched into rock are called _____.

3. The outside line of a drawing is called the _____.

B Circle the letter next to the correct answer for items 4–7. Write the answer to item 8.

4. Rock art is _____ form of art.
   A. a very old   **B.** a new   **C.** an unrealistic

5. Rock art is found _____.
   A. in the U.S.A. only   **B.** in Europe only   **C.** in many parts of the world

6. Rock art often shows pictures of _____.
   A. inventions   **B.** seasons   **C.** animals

7. What does rock art show about the people who created it?
   A. They valued animals and studied them carefully.
   B. Animals were not important in their lives.
   C. They did not hunt or fish very much.

8. Look at the oxen in *Art Print 5, Sodbuster: San Isidro*. Suppose an artist scratched an image of an ox on a rock. Name key details that would help viewers know the animal right away.

_____

_____

TEACHER NOTE | Display *Art Print 5* while students complete this page.

Write About an Animal Encounter

 Plan and Write   Choose an animal portrayed in Lesson 1 (turtle, rhinoceros, or rattlesnake) or another animal that interests you. Write a story about an imaginary encounter with that animal. Start by deciding on the setting and the characters. Then choose a problem to be solved in the story. Think about a problem that might happen when you meet the animal. Then think about events that could lead to a solution. Use colorful details to make your writing more interesting. Use the story map below to plan your story, and write it on a separate piece of paper.

Setting:	Characters:

Problem:

Beginning:

Middle:

Solution:

End:

Name _____

Vocabulary and Concepts

landscapes
foreground
background
middle ground

A Label the drawing with words from the box. Then complete the sentence.

1. _____

2. _____

3. _____

4. Artists often paint _____

   to show very large areas.

B Read the questions below and write the answers.

5. Imagine you are painting a landscape of a desert. What details might you include to

   help show what the place is like? _____

   _____

6. Describe how artists use size to make some objects in a painting look closer than others.

   _____

   _____

7. Describe how artists place objects in paintings to make some look closer than others.

   _____

   _____

Write About Likes and Dislikes

 Plan and Write   Suppose you could visit one of the regions shown in the paintings in Lesson 2—the high plains, a forest and mountains in winter, or the sea coast. Choose the region you would like to visit. Write a composition for your teacher telling both what you like about this region and what you do not like about it. Be sure to explain your ideas in detail. Use the organizer below to plan your composition, and write it on a separate sheet of paper.

First, name which region you would like to visit. Write a catchy opening sentence.

Next, list three things you like about the region, starting with the most important. Extend each detail with a reason.
 	
Detail 1:
 	
    Reason:
 	
Detail 2:
 	
    Reason:
 	
Detail 3:
 	
    Reason:

Now list three things you do not like. Again, add details and reasons.
Detail 1:
 	
    Reason:
 	
Detail 2:
 	
    Reason:
 	
Detail 3:
 	
    Reason:

Finally, write a conclusion that summarizes the good points and bad points.

Harcourt Brace School Publishers

Name _____

Vocabulary and Concepts

> **proportion**
> **point of view**
> **shape**

A Write a word from the box next to the meaning it matches.

1. the place from which a view is seen _____

2. square, triangle, or circle _____

3. the size of one thing compared to the size of another _____

B Answer each question with a complete sentence.

4. Look at *Art Print 4, The Boating Party*. What was the artist's point of view when she painted this picture?

_____

_____

5. Name three shapes that the artist used in the painting.

_____

_____

6. Describe how the artist made the houses in the background look far away.

_____

_____

7. Describe how the artist made the man rowing the boat look closer than the woman.

_____

_____

TEACHER NOTE Display *Art Print 4* while students complete this page.

Harcourt Brace School Publishers

Vocabulary and Concepts　　　　GRADE 4 • ASSESSMENT PROGRAM • LESSON 3　　**7**

Write to Persuade

 Plan and Write   Imagine that your class could take a trip to the mountains shown in Lesson 3, or to another outdoor place. Write a composition for your teacher to convince him or her that the class trip is a good idea. Include reasons to go on the trip and explain your ideas in detail. Use the organizer below to plan your composition, and write it on a separate piece of paper.

Write the beginning.

Opinion statement:
One sentence to grab your teacher's interest:

Write the middle. Write at least three reasons that support your opinion. For each reason, give at least one fact, or give an emotional appeal that would make your teacher really want to take you on the trip. Arrange your reasons from most important to least important.

Reason 1:
Why:
Reason 2:
Why:
Reason 3:
Why:

Write the end.

A summary of your opinion:
A call for action:

Harcourt Brace School Publishers

Name _____

Vocabulary and Concepts

A **Circle the letter next to the phrase that best completes each sentence.**

1. **Organic** shapes _____.
   A. are rounded and uneven, like shapes found in nature
   B. do not appear in nature
   C. are square and very even

2. A color's **value** is _____.
   A. how much it costs
   B. how light or dark it is
   C. where it is placed in a painting

3. **Contrast** is _____.
   A. the size of an object
   B. the shape of an object
   C. the difference between two things

B **Use the picture to answer each question.**

4. What can you see in a close-up view of a starfish that you cannot see in a view from far

   away? _____

   _____

5. Is the starfish's shape organic? Explain. _____

   _____

6. Suppose you were going to paint a picture of a group of starfish together on a rock.
   How could you use different values of color to make certain starfish stand out?

   _____

   _____

Harcourt Brace School Publishers

Write About a Natural Object

 Plan and Write   Imagine you have found a special object in nature such as a shell, flower, or unusual rock. Write a paragraph for your teacher, describing its features. Be sure to write about your ideas in detail. Use the organizer below to plan your composition, and write it on a separate piece of paper.

First, write a topic sentence telling what the object is and where you found it.

| |
| |
| |

Next, write details about the object. Use specific adjectives to make your writing more interesting.

What it looks like:
What it feels like:
Does it have a smell? If so, describe it.
Does it make a sound? If so, describe it.

(When you write your paragraph, be sure to group details that belong together.)

Finally, write a conclusion that summarizes why the object is unique.

| |
| |
| |

Name _____

Vocabulary and Concepts

A Write the letter of each definition on the right on the line next to the word or phrase it matches.

1. natural environment _____

2. diorama _____

3. figure _____

4. space _____

A. the shape of a person, animal, or thing

B. the place where an animal lives

C. distance, area, or depth in a work of art

D. a scene in which three-dimensional models are displayed against a background

B Answer the questions using complete sentences.

5. When artists paint pictures of wild animals, what do they often show in the

background? _____

_____

6. Both of the paintings in Lesson 5 are of animals. How did each artist make the animal

he painted look at home? _____

_____

7. Suppose you were going to make a diorama of a seal in its natural environment. What would you paint in the background? What figures would you place in the foreground?

_____

_____

8. How would the background in a painting of a polar bear be different from the

background in a painting of a monkey that lives in a tropical forest? _____

_____

_____

Harcourt Brace School Publishers

Write About Winter

 Plan and Write Think of the snowy scene in Lesson 5. Write a composition for your teacher explaining both what you like about winter and what you do not like about it. Be sure to explain your ideas in detail. Use the organizer below to plan your composition, and write it on a separate piece of paper.

First, name your topic. Write a catchy opening sentence.

Next, list three things you like about winter, starting with the most important. Add a reason for each detail.

Detail 1:

Reason:

Detail 2:

Reason:

Detail 3:

Reason:

Now list three things you do not like. Again, add details and reasons.

Detail 1:

Reason:

Detail 2:

Reason:

Detail 3:

Reason:

Finally, write an ending that sums up the main ideas.

Name _____

Vocabulary and Concepts

overlap
still life
center of interest

 A **Write each word from the box next to its definition.**

1. a picture of an arrangement of natural and _____
   human-made objects

2. to cover up part of a shape with another shape _____

3. the part of a painting that stands out _____

B **Circle the letter next to the correct answer.**

4. Look at *Art Print 2, Still Life*. What is the center of interest in the painting?
   A. the large yellow cheese   **B.** the grapes   **C.** the tablecloths

5. Which of these two objects overlap in the picture?
   A. the cheese and the apple
   B. the knife and the plate
   C. the glass and the grapes

6. What is an important first step in creating a still life?
   A. carefully arranging the objects to be painted
   B. placing objects outdoors
   C. buying expensive objects to be painted

7. Why do you think the artist painted this still life?
   A. to show what he had for lunch
   B. to show what his house looked like
   C. to show the beauty of ordinary things

TEACHER NOTE   Display *Art Print 2* while students complete this page.

Write About How to Care for a Pet

 Plan and Write   Suppose a friend has just gotten a new pet, like one of the puppies pictured in the painting in Lesson 6. Write directions explaining how to feed the pet or give the pet a bath, or how to do some other chore related to caring for the animal. List the steps that your friend would need to follow to complete the chore. Be sure to explain the steps in order. Be clear and detailed so another person can follow the steps. Use the organizer below to plan your composition. Then write it on a separate piece of paper.

How-To Topic: (Write a topic sentence that tells what you will be explaining.)	**Materials Needed:**

Step 1:

(Remember to use time-order words such as *first*.)

Step 2:

(Use time-order words such as *next* and *then*.)

Step 3:

Step 4:

(Use time-order words such as *finally* or *last*.)

Harcourt Brace School Publishers

Name _____

A Read each phrase. Find the best meaning for each underlined art vocabulary term. Fill in the circle for your answer.

1. the value of a color
   A. cost
   B. lightness or darkness
   C. amount of green
   D. beauty

2. the contrast in the colors
   A. brightness
   B. darkness
   C. difference
   D. similarity

3. the background of the painting
   A. part in the distance
   B. picture frame
   C. figures in front
   D overlapping

4. the petroglyph of the tiger
   A. paws
   B. rock painting
   C. sculpture
   D. mural

5. painting a still life
   A. arrangement of objects
   B. person who stands still
   C. flower
   D. colorful picture

ANSWERS

1. A B C D
2. A B C D
3. A B C D
4. A B C D
5. A B C D

B Write the letter of the word or phrase on the right that best completes each sentence.

A. center of interest
B. outline
C. landscapes
D. point of view
E. space

6. Artists often paint _____ showing large areas of land.

7. The viewer's eye is drawn to a painting's _____.

8. The artist first drew the _____ of the shape and then shaded the center.

9. You can get new ideas about a familiar object by looking at it from a different _____.

10. The _____ in a painting can be the open areas in which objects are not shown.

TEACHER NOTE Display *Art Prints 1, 2,* and *9* and several additional *Art Prints* while students complete this review.

C **Write or draw the answers to the questions. Make your drawings on another sheet of paper.**

11. Long before people used paper and pencil, how did early artists create pictures of

animals? _____

12. Draw a simple outline of a turtle.

13.–14. Look at *Art Print 9, Gargoyle*. What is in the foreground? in the background?

_____

_____

15.–16. Make two simple sketches of an object from two different points of view.

17. Look at *Art Print 1, Hunt's Vase*. What is the center of interest? _____

_____

18. What organic shapes do you see? _____

_____

19. Look at *Art Print 2, Still Life*. Did the artist use placement or size to show that

some objects are closer than others? Explain your answer. _____

_____

20. Find an artwork displayed in your classroom that fits well in this unit, "Beauty All Around." Write the artwork's title and artist and explain why you chose it.

_____

_____

Harcourt Brace School Publishers

Name _____

Vocabulary and Concepts

A Circle the letter next to the word or phrase that best completes each sentence.

1. A **portrait** shows _____.
   A. movement in the water   B. a natural scene   C. what a person looks like

2. A **contour** line is _____.
   A. a line between overlapping objects
   B. the outer edge of a figure
   C. a line carved in rock

3. The **features** of a face include its _____.
   A. eyes, nose, mouth, and ears   B. colors and shadows   C. movement

B Answer the questions using complete sentences.

4. Why do artists paint portraits?_____

   _____

5. What can you learn about a person from his or her portrait? _____

   _____

   _____

6. How do artists use proportion when they paint portraits?_____

   _____

   _____

Write a Character Sketch

 Plan and Write   A portrait is one way to show the likeness of a real person. A character sketch is another way to do this. Write a character sketch of an interesting or special person you know for your teacher. Include details that show how the person acts, what the person looks like, and what talents or special skills the person has. Use the organizer below to plan your character sketch, and write it on a separate piece of paper.

First, write a topic sentence naming the person you are going to describe. Be sure to include the relationship of the person to you (for example, friend, brother, or sister).

Details about how the person looks:

Details about how the person acts:

Details about the person's special talents or skills:

Finally, write a conclusion that summarizes what this person is like and why he or she is interesting or special to you.

Name _____

Vocabulary and Concepts

profile
texture
relief sculpture

A Write a word from the box to complete each sentence.

1. A _____ is a raised design carved from a surface.

2. Look at the picture of the quarter. George

   Washington's _____ faces left.

3. Wavy lines carved into the quarter show the _____ of Washington's hair.

B Write *true* or *false* on the line next to each statement. If a statement is *false*, rewrite it so it is correct.

4. Relief sculptures often show what real people look like. _____

   _____

   _____

5. All relief sculptures are the same size. _____

   _____

6. Relief sculptures are flat, like paintings. _____

   _____

7. Relief sculptures can show the texture of materials such as hair and cloth. _____

   _____

   _____

Write a Comparison

▶ **Plan and Write**   Coins are some of the smallest examples of relief sculpture. Write a composition for your teacher comparing a coin with paper money. Write two paragraphs that compare and contrast the two kinds of money. Be sure to include plenty of details in your comparison. Use the chart below to plan your composition. Write your composition on another piece of paper.

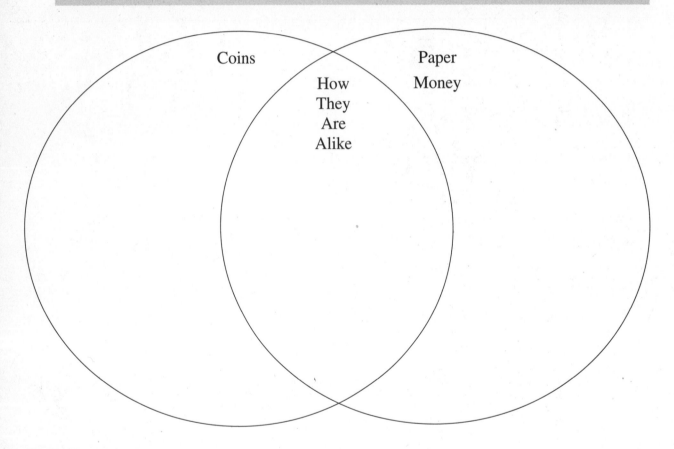

Coins   How They Are Alike   Paper Money

Tips for Comparing

1. Begin the first paragraph with a topic sentence that tells what you are comparing. Give two or three details that tell how coins and paper money are alike. (Use signal words such as *both*.)

2. Begin the second paragraph with a topic sentence, too. Then give two or three details that tell how coins and paper money are different.

3. In the last sentence, sum up how coins and paper money are alike and different.

Harcourt Brace School Publishers

Name _____

Vocabulary and Concepts

 Complete each sentence with a word from the box.

triangle
model
cube
abstract

1. A(n) _____ painting does not show a lifelike picture of something.

2. A(n) _____ has three sides.

3. A square block is a(n) _____.

4. The _____ for the portrait in Lesson 9 was a real princess.

B **Answer questions 5–7 using complete sentences. For item 8, circle the letter next to the correct answer.**

5. How is Picasso's portrait of the princess in Lesson 9 different from the original

painting?_____

_____

6. How are the two paintings alike? _____

_____

7. Name two shapes Picasso used in his abstract painting. _____

_____

8. What do artists experiment with when painting an abstract portrait?
   A. color, shape, and proportion   C. natural and human-made objects
   B. history   D. detailed landscapes

Write a Letter to a Princess

 Plan and Write Write a friendly letter to a princess such as the one pictured in Lesson 9. Think about what you would like to tell her about yourself and what you want to know about her. Be sure to include the five parts of a friendly letter. Write your ideas clearly and in detail. Use the organizer below to plan your letter. Then write it on a separate sheet of paper.

	Heading Your address:
Greeting Dear Princess _____, 　　　Write a name for the princess here.	Today's date:

First paragraph: Introduce yourself to the princess. Include interesting details about yourself, such as where you live and where you go to school.

Detail 1:

Detail 2:

Detail 3:

Second paragraph: Ask the princess some specific questions that you have about her life, such as where she lives and what she does every day.

Question 1:

Question 2:

Question 3:

Last paragraph: Think of a way to end your letter.

Closing
Your friend,

_____
Write your **signature** here.

B
O
D
Y

o
f

L
E
T
T
E
R

Name _____

Vocabulary and Concepts

| tints |
| shades |
| monochromatic |
| mood |

A Complete each sentence with a word from the box.

1. A picture with one color is _____.

2. Colors made darker by adding black are _____.

3. Colors made lighter by adding white are _____.

4. A feeling or emotion is a _____.

B Answer questions 5 and 6 using complete sentences. For items 7 and 8, write the correct word or phrase on the lines.

5. Think about the paintings you studied in Lesson 10: *Poor People on the Seashore (The Tragedy)* by Pablo Picasso and *El Pan Nuestro* by Diego Rivera. Contrast the two paintings by answering these questions: How are the colors different in the two paintings? How are the moods different? _____

   _____

   _____

6. Look at *Art Print 3, The Gourmet*. Does this painting have a monochromatic color scheme? Why or why not? _____

   _____

7. Is the main color in *The Gourmet* a warm or a cool color? _____

8. By using one main color in a painting, an artist may be trying to set a

   _____.

TEACHER NOTE Display *Art Print 3* while students complete this page.

Name _____

Write About How to Make a Favorite Dish

 Plan and Write One of the pictures in Lesson 10 shows a family about to share a meal. Suppose you want to teach a friend how to make one of your favorite things to eat. Choose something that you know how to make. List any ingredients needed. Be sure to explain the steps in order. Be clear and detailed so your friend can follow the steps. Use the organizer below to plan your directions, and write them on a separate sheet of paper.

How-To Topic:
(Write a topic sentence that tells what you will be explaining.)

Ingredients:

Step 1:

(Remember to use time-order words such as *first*.)

Step 2:

(Use time-order words such as *next* and *then*.)

Step 3:

Step 4:

(Use time-order words such as *finally* or *last*.)

Name _____

Vocabulary and Concepts

A Circle the letter next to the phrase that best completes each sentence.

1. The word **unity** describes the way parts of a painting _____.
   A. are tied together   **B.** look different   **C.** match real life

2. Artists create **rhythm** by painting _____.
   A. a solid background
   B. shades or tints
   C. patterns of shapes and colors that seem to move

3. If a color is **repeated** in a painting, it appears _____.
   A. one time only   **B.** more than once   **C.** in a dark shade

B Write complete sentences to answer these questions.

4. Look at *Art Print 12, The Persistence of Memory* by Salvador Dalí. What image is

   repeated in this painting? _____

   _____

5. How did Salvador Dalí use color to create unity in this painting? _____

   _____

6. Look at *Art Print 8, Hydria: Women Sorting Wool.* How do the colors on the vase help

   give it a sense of unity? _____

   _____

Harcourt Brace School Publishers

| **TEACHER NOTE** | Display *Art Prints 8* and *12* while students complete this page. |

Write About a Favorite Activity

 Plan and Write   Lesson 11 showed a painting of dancers. Think of an activity you enjoy, such as dancing, playing a sport, or belonging to a club. Write a composition trying to convince a friend that he or she would enjoy that activity. Include reasons to take part in the activity and explain your ideas in detail. Use the organizer below to plan your composition, and write it on a separate piece of paper.

1. Write the beginning.

Opinion statement that will grab your reader's interest:

2. Write the middle. Write at least three reasons that support your opinion. For each reason, give at least one fact, or give an emotional appeal that would make your reader really want to try the activity that you recommend. Arrange your reasons from most important to least important.

Reason 1:
Fact:
Reason 2:
Fact:
Reason 3:
Fact:

3. Write your conclusion.

A summary of your opinion:
What your reader should do:

Name _____

Vocabulary and Concepts

> movement
> horizontal line
> diagonal line

A Label the drawing with words from the box. Then complete the sentence.

1. _____

2. _____

3. The action lines in this picture help

   show _____.

B Write *true or false* on the line next to each statement. If a statement is *false*, rewrite it so it is correct.

4. Action lines are always horizontal. _____

   _____

5. A subject in a painting can show movement if the subject's body is slanted to the right

   or left. _____

   _____

6. People's legs and arms can be drawn with diagonal lines to show movement. _____

   _____

7. Look at *Art Print 4, The Boating Party*. In this painting there are no diagonal lines

   suggesting movement. _____

   _____

| **TEACHER NOTE** | Display *Art Print 4* while students complete this page. |

Write About How to Play a Game

 Plan and Write   A picture in Lesson 12 shows a group of boys playing an outdoor game called Snap the Whip. Suppose you want to teach a friend how to play your favorite indoor or outdoor game. Write a how-to paragraph explaining how to play the game. Be clear and detailed so your friend can play the game correctly. Use the organizer below to plan your paragraph, and write it on a separate piece of paper.

Game: (Write a topic sentence about the game you will be explaining.)	**Equipment Needed:**

Step 1:

(Remember to use time-order words such as *first*.)

▼

Step 2:

(Use time-order words such as *next* and *then*.)

▼

Step 3:

▼

Step 4:

(Use time-order words such as *finally* or *last*.)

Harcourt Brace School Publishers

Name _____

A Write the letter of each definition on the right next to the word it matches.

1. contour _____   **A.** slanting

2. shades _____   **B.** outline of a figure

3. diagonal _____   **C.** shape with three sides

4. monochromatic _____   **D.** having one color

5. triangle _____   **E.** colors darkened by adding black

B Find the word or phrase that best completes each sentence. Fill in the circle for your answer.

ANSWERS

6. (A) (B) (C) (D)
7. (A) (B) (C) (D)
8. (A) (B) (C) (D)
9. (A) (B) (C) (D)
10. (A) (B) (C) (D)

6. _____ are pictures of real people.
   A. Shades   **C.** Portraits
   B. Still lifes   **D.** Landscapes

7. Repeated lines, shapes, or colors can create _____ in a painting.
   A. shades   **B.** contour   **C.** rhythm   **D.** triangles

8. _____ are carved out of a surface.
   A. Relief sculptures   **B.** Landscapes   **C.** Shades   **D.** Portraits

9. _____ are not lifelike.
   A. Abstract paintings   **B.** Landscape paintings   **C.** Still lifes   **D.** Portraits

10. Tying parts of an artwork together creates _____ .
    A. texture   **B.** unity   **C.** color   **D.** tints

TEACHER NOTE Display *Art Prints 2, 5,* and *6* while students complete this review.

Name _____

C   **Write or draw the answers to the questions.**

11.   Draw a person's *profile* on a separate sheet of paper.

12. On a separate sheet of paper, draw a simple sketch of a moving figure. Include lines that show movement.

13. What kind of artwork might an artist create to show what a specific person looks like?

    _____

14. How is an abstract portrait different from a realistic portrait? _____

    _____

15. Describe how an artist can use colors to create a happy mood in a painting.

    _____

16. Look at *Art Print 2, Still Life.* List three shapes that you see in the painting.

    _____

17. Find an object in *Art Print 2* that has different values of color. Identify the object and its

    colors. _____

18. Look at *Art Print 6, Desserts.* How did the artist create unity in this picture?

    _____

19. Look at *Art Print 5, Sodbuster: San Isidro.* Do you see any diagonal lines that show

    movement in this sculpture? If so, where do you see them? _____

    _____

20. Find an artwork displayed in your classroom that fits well in this unit, "Picturing People." Name the artwork's title and artist and explain why you chose it.

    _____

    _____

Name _____

Vocabulary and Concepts

A Write the letter of each word on the right in the blank where it belongs.

1. Something that is _____ has height, length, and depth.   **A.** sculptures

2. Many _____ are carved out of stone.   **B.** three-dimensional

3. An object that is _____ is not moving.   **C.** still

B Circle the letter next to the best answer for questions 4 and 5. Then answer questions 6 and 7 in complete sentences.

4. What do the sculptures in Lesson 13 reveal about horses?
   A. Horses are happiest in their natural environment.
   B. Horses can be trained to perform.
   C. Horses have been important to people for many centuries.

5. What is the clearest way to portray a horse in motion?
   A. Show the horse's front or back legs in the air.
   B. Show the horse's four legs straight on the ground.
   C. Show a person sitting in the horse's saddle.

6. Look at *Art Print 5, Sodbuster: San Isidro.* How can you tell that this work of art is a

   sculpture? _____

   _____

7. Do you think the oxen in this sculpture are still or in motion? How can you tell?

   _____

   _____

TEACHER NOTE Display *Art Print 5* while students complete this page.

Harcourt Brace School Publishers

Write a Description of an Animal

▶ **Plan and Write**   Lesson 13 showed three different sculptures of horses. Think of what your favorite animal is like, and write a description of it. Use descriptive phrases and action words so your reader can picture the animal clearly. In your last sentence, tell reasons why the animal is your favorite. Use the organizer below to plan your composition, and write it on a separate piece of paper.

1. Write the beginning.

Introduce the animal:

2. Write the middle. Use the web to think of descriptive phrases and action words.

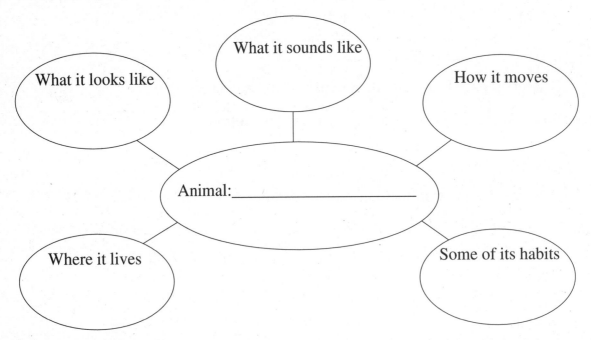

3. Write your conclusion.

Tell why the animal is your favorite:

Harcourt Brace School Publishers

Name _____

Vocabulary and Concepts

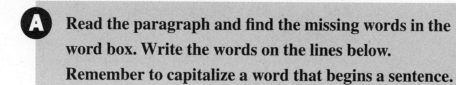

frame
comic strips
characters
cartoonist

A Read the paragraph and find the missing words in the
word box. Write the words on the lines below.
Remember to capitalize a word that begins a sentence.

 <u>1.</u>___ tell stories in words and pictures. You can read them in the daily newspaper.
A <u>2.</u>___ is the person who draws the pictures and writes the words. The animals and
people in the stories are called <u>3.</u>___. The artist draws each part of the story inside a
box called a <u>4.</u>___. These boxes help readers follow the events in order.

1. _____   3. _____

2. _____   4. _____

B Write the answer to each question. Use complete sentences.

5. How can a cartoonist show how a character is feeling? _____

_____

6. How can a cartoonist show that a character is moving? _____

_____

7. Are comic strips created only to make people laugh? Explain your answer.

_____

_____

8. Think about the comic you read in Lesson 14. What message do you think Charles

Schulz was giving readers in this comic? _____

_____

Vocabulary and Concepts

Name _____

Write a Story About a Cartoon Character

 Plan and Write   Choose a cartoon character from Lesson 14 (Snoopy or Woodstock, the bird) or another comic strip character you like. Write a story about that character. Imagine that he or she could attend your school for a day. Tell about an interesting or unusual event that might happen. Use action words to make the writing more interesting. Use the story map below to plan your story, and write it on a separate piece of paper.

Setting:	Characters:

Problem:

IDEA BANK
- win a game in the last second
- find a lost object
- save a playground

▼

Beginning:

▼

Middle:

▼

Solution:

▼

End:

Harcourt Brace School Publishers

Name _____

Vocabulary and Concepts

 A Write a word or phrase from the box in each blank below.

symbol
coat of
arms
state seal

1. _____

2. _____

3. The dove is a _____ of peace.

B Choose the best answer and fill in the circle of your choice.

4. Coats of arms are about _____ years old.

   A. 80
   B. 800

   C. 180
   D. 18

5. Coats of arms were first used _____.

   A. to tell about the history of a particular place

   B. to stand for important ideas

   C. to help soldiers recognize their knights in battle

   D. to tell about family histories

6. Artists use symbols to _____.

   A. show when events happened
   B. show who the current leader is

   C. stand for important ideas
   D. tell about important battles

7. State seals often _____.

   A. tell about the history of the state
   B. identify a particular family

   C. explain important laws
   D. show who the current governor is

ANSWERS

4. Ⓐ Ⓑ Ⓒ Ⓓ
5. Ⓐ Ⓑ Ⓒ Ⓓ
6. Ⓐ Ⓑ Ⓒ Ⓓ
7. Ⓐ Ⓑ Ⓒ Ⓓ

Harcourt Brace School Publishers

Write About Your State

Plan and Write In Lesson 15 you learned about the importance of state seals. Think of why your state is a great place to live. Write a composition trying to convince a friend or relative who lives in another state to move to your state. Include detailed reasons why a person should live in your state. Use the organizer below to plan your composition, and write it on a separate piece of paper.

Write the beginning.

Opinion statement that will grab your reader's interest:

Write the middle. Think about how to convince your reader. Write at least three reasons that support your opinion. For each reason, give at least one fact or emotional appeal. Arrange your reasons from most important to least important.

Reason 1:   Fact:
Reason 2:   Fact:
Reason 3:   Fact:

Write your conclusion.

Your opinion, in different words: **What your reader should do:**

Harcourt Brace School Publishers

Name _____

Vocabulary and Concepts

stamp
Pop Art
print

 A Match each word in the box with its meaning. Write the words on the lines.

1. This style of art features everyday objects such as soup cans. _____

2. This art form is made by pressing one design onto paper again and again.

   _____

3. You spread ink onto this and then press it onto paper to make a shape.

   _____

B For items 4–6, circle the letter next to the correct answer. Write a sentence to answer item 7.

4. Which object might be the subject of a Pop Art painting?
   A. a rainbow   B. a box of pencils   C. an oak tree

5. What everyday objects are the subjects of the paintings in Lesson 16?
   A. soup cans and soda bottles   B. pencils and stamps   C. stencils and ink

6. What is Pop Art's main message?
   A. Art should be simple.
   B. Any common object can become art.
   C. Art should come from nature.

7. Look at *Art Print 6, Desserts*. Do you think this painting is an example of Pop Art?

   Why or why not? _____

   _____

TEACHER NOTE Display *Art Print 6* while students complete this page.

Write a Description of Objects in a Time Capsule

 Plan and Write   Lesson 16 showed paintings of common objects from the modern world. Suppose you had to choose four everyday objects to place in a time capsule that will be opened 100 years from now. The objects you select should help someone in the future understand what life is like today. Write a letter to go with the objects in the time capsule. Tell what objects you have put into the time capsule and why you have chosen each one. Use the organizer below to plan your letter, and write it on a separate piece of paper.

	Heading
Greeting Dear future friend,	Your address: Today's date:
What is in the time capsule Object 1:	**Why I have included it**
Object 2:	
Object 3:	
Object 4:	
Last paragraph: Think of a way to end your letter.	
Closing Your friend, _____ Write your **signature** here.	

B O D Y o f L E T T E R

Name _____

Vocabulary and Concepts

glow
scene
cityscape

A **Complete each sentence with a word from the box.**

1. A _____ shows a picture of a city.

2. A soft light is called a _____.

3. A _____ is a picture of a place.

B **Answer each question below.**

4. Compare *Art Print 4, The Boating Party*, with *Art Print 9, Gargoyle*. Which shows a

   cityscape? _____

5. The photograph *Gargoyle* makes viewers feel that the city is _____.
   A. a warm, inviting place   **C.** a cold, forbidding place
   B. full of friendly people   **D.** colorful and beautiful

6. What shapes would you expect to see more of in a cityscape, geometric shapes or

   organic shapes? Why?   _____

   _____

7. Think about a cityscape painted during the daytime and another painted at night. Where

   do you think the light would probably come from in each painting? _____

   _____

   _____

TEACHER NOTE Display *Art Prints 4* and *9* while students complete this page.

Write About Cities

 Plan and Write Write a composition for your teacher explaining both what you like about cities and what you do not like about them. Be sure to explain your ideas in detail. Use the organizer below to plan your composition, and write it on a separate piece of paper.

First, name your topic. Write a catchy opening sentence.

Next, list three things you like about cities, starting with the most important. Add a reason for each detail.

Detail 1:

Reason:

Detail 2:

Reason:

Detail 3:

Reason:

Now list three things you do not like. Again, add details and reasons.

Detail 1:

Reason:

Detail 2:

Reason:

Detail 3:

Reason:

Finally, write an ending that summarizes the good points and bad points.

Name _____

Vocabulary and Concepts

A   **Write the letter of each phrase on the right next to the word it matches.**

1. style _____

2. realistic _____

3. Impressionistic _____

4. stylized _____

A. shows objects as simple shapes without many details

B. the way in which an artist chooses to show a subject

C. shows a fleeting impression or view of a scene

D. shows things as they look in the real world

B   **Write the answers to the questions. Use complete sentences.**

5. What type of vehicle is shown in each of the paintings in Lesson 18? How are the paintings alike? How are they different?

   _____

   _____

6. Look at *Art Print 2, Still Life*. Is this painting realistic or stylized? Explain your answer.

   _____

   _____

7. Look at *Art Print 4, The Boating Party*. How do you think this painting would look different if it were done in a realistic style?

   _____

   _____

8. How would a stylized picture of a car be different from a realistic picture of a car?

   _____

   _____

TEACHER NOTE   Display *Art Prints 2* and *4* while students complete this page.

Name _____

Write to Persuade

 Plan and Write   Lesson 18 showed pictures of trains. Think about your favorite way to travel. Write a persuasive paragraph for your parents trying to convince them to use that method of transportation the next time your family travels. Include detailed reasons to travel that way. Use the organizer to plan your paragraph, and write it on a separate piece of paper.

Write the beginning.

One sentence to grab your parents' interest:
Opinion statement:

Write the middle. Think about how to convince your parents. Write at least three reasons to support your opinion. For each reason, give at least one fact or emotional appeal. Arrange your reasons from most important to least important.

Reason 1: Fact:
Reason 2: Fact:
Reason 3: Fact:

Write your conclusion.

Your opinion, in different words:
What your parents should do:

Name _____

A **Choose the best answer and fill in the circle for your choice.**

1. a picture of a place
   A. style   C. frame
   B. profile   D. scene

2. a three-dimensional artwork
   A. cityscape   C. stencil
   B. print   D. sculpture

3. the special way an artist shows a subject
   A. style   B. symbol   C. Pop Art   D. scene

4. like real life
   A. stylized   B. realistic   C. abstract   D. Impressionistic

5. something that stands for an idea
   A. print   B. stamp   C. symbol   D. scene

ANSWERS

1. Ⓐ Ⓑ Ⓒ Ⓓ
2. Ⓐ Ⓑ Ⓒ Ⓓ
3. Ⓐ Ⓑ Ⓒ Ⓓ
4. Ⓐ Ⓑ Ⓒ Ⓓ
5. Ⓐ Ⓑ Ⓒ Ⓓ

B **Complete each sentence with a word from the box.**

cityscape
comic strip
stamp
print
Pop Art
three-dimensional

6. A _____ can be used to make
   many copies of the same image.

7. A statue isn't flat. It is _____.

8. A _____ shows a view of a
   city, such as a busy street with many tall buildings.

9. An artist can use ink and a rubber stamp to make a _____.

10. A _____ tells stories with pictures and words.

11. A painting of a toothpaste tube might be an example of _____.

C   **Write or draw the answers to the questions.**

12. On a separate sheet of paper, draw a simple coat of arms.

13. Look at *Art Print 11, Lever No. 3*. What kind of artwork is this? _____

14. How can a cartoonist show movement? _____

15. What do state seals and coats of arms have in common? _____

_____

16. Look at *Art Print 12, The Persistence of Memory*. What image might be a symbol of

time? _____

17. How can artists show their feelings about a subject through their work? _____

_____

18. Compare *Art Print 2, Still Life* and *Art Print 6, Desserts*. How are the subjects of the

painting similar? How are the styles of the paintings different? _____

_____

19. Describe how an artist can use light to show a mood in a painting of a place, such as a

city. _____

_____

20. Find an artwork displayed in your classroom that fits well in this unit, "Expressions."
    Write the artwork's title and artist and explain why you chose it. _____

_____

_____

TEACHER NOTE   Display *Art Prints 2, 6, 11*, and *12* while students complete this page.

Harcourt Brace School Publishers

Name _____

Vocabulary and Concepts

A Write the letter of each definition on the right on the line next to the word it matches.

1. mask _____   **A.** a number of different kinds

2. variety _____   **B.** related to a formal act done to celebrate a special occasion

3. traditional _____   **C.** handed down through many generations

4. ceremonial _____   **D.** a covering worn over the face

B Choose the best answer and fill in the circle of your choice.

5. What animal pictured in Lesson 19 symbolizes strength and courage for the Mayas of Mexico?

   A. the jaguar   **C.** the lion

   B. the toucan   **D.** the snake

6. Which group is most likely to wear ceremonial masks?

   A. children listening to a story

   B. leaders speaking to a crowd

   C. people watching a performance

   D. performers acting out a story

ANSWERS
4. Ⓐ Ⓑ Ⓒ Ⓓ
5. Ⓐ Ⓑ Ⓒ Ⓓ
6. Ⓐ Ⓑ Ⓒ Ⓓ
7. Ⓐ Ⓑ Ⓒ Ⓓ

7. Which statement below is true about masks in general?

   A. They are worn only in Africa and Mexico.

   B. They are worn only while dancing.

   C. They are worn only at parties.

   D. Nearly every group of people has made and used them.

8. When did people start using masks?

   A. in the 1960s   **C.** in ancient times

   B. in the 1800s   **D.** in modern times

Name _____

Write a Story About a Jaguar

 Plan and Write The jaguar mask in Lesson 19 can be used to tell stories. Write a story about the jaguar and two other animals. Think of a problem these characters might have. Next, think about events that could lead to a solution to the problem. Tell the story events in order. Use the story map below to plan your story. Then write it on a separate sheet of paper.

Setting:	Main Characters:
Where:	
When:	Other Characters:

Problem:

IDEA BANK:

- have a contest to see who is the most clever
- plan a special celebration for an animal
- deal with a natural disaster, such as a fire or a hurricane
- solve a jungle mystery

Beginning:

(Remember to use time-order words such as *first* or *one day*.)

Middle:

Event 1:

Event 2:

Event 3:

(Use time-order words such as *then, later on*, and *next*.)

Solution:

(Think of a clever way for the jaguar to solve the problem.)

End:

(Use time-order words such as *finally*.)

Name _____

Vocabulary and Concepts

| positive shapes |
| implied |
| actual |
| negative shapes |

A **Complete each sentence with a word or phrase from the box. Remember to capitalize a word that begins a sentence.**

1. The empty space in a painting or other artwork creates _____.

2. _____ lines are hidden outlines.

3. Outlines you can see are called _____ lines.

4. _____ are the shapes of the things being shown in a work of art.

B **Look at the picture. Answer the questions using complete sentences.**

5. The elephant's eye is shown with a negative shape. What other part of its body is

    shown with a negative shape? _____

    _____

6. What other detail is shown with negative shapes? _____

    _____

7. Do you see *actual* lines or *implied* lines where the elephant's feet touch the ground?

    Explain. _____

    _____

Harcourt Brace School Publishers

Write a Personal Narrative

 Plan and Write   In many cultures the rooster is a symbol of new beginnings. Write a personal narrative for your teacher telling about a new beginning in your life. You might want to write about joining a team, learning to play a musical instrument, or your first year at a new school. Be sure to describe the events in the order in which they happened. Include colorful details that show why this experience was special for you. Use the chart below to plan your composition. Write your composition on another piece of paper.

Beginning

First, tell what you started. Write an opening sentence that grabs the reader's attention.

Middle

Next, list the events that happened in the correct order. Include a detailed description of each event. Also describe how you felt during the experience.

Event 1:

   Description/Details:

Event 2:

   Description/Details:

Event 3:

   Description/Details:

Ending

Finally, write a conclusion that tells how the experience ended. Sum up the reasons why this experience was special for you.

Harcourt Brace School Publishers

Name _____

Vocabulary and Concepts

> potter
> pottery
> kiln
> vessels

 A Read the paragraph and find the missing words in the word box. Write the words on the lines below.

Bowls and jars are called __1.__ because they hold things. Bowls and jars made out of hardened clay are called __2.__. First the __3.__ shapes the clay and lets it dry. Then the clay is baked in a very hot oven called a __4.__.

1. _____   3. _____

2. _____   4. _____

B Write *true* or *false* on the line next to each statement. If a statement is *false*, rewrite it so it is correct.

5. Pottery is found only in museums. _____

_____

_____

6. Pottery is an ancient form of art. _____

_____

_____

7. Pottery is only used for special occasions, not for everyday living. _____

_____

_____

8. The image of the bear is a Pueblo symbol for water. _____

_____

_____

Write a How-to Paragraph

 Plan and Write   The skill of pottery making is often passed down through generations. Think of an important skill you have learned from an older family member, such as how to ride a bike or how to make something. Write directions for a younger friend or relative explaining how to do that. Be sure to list all the important steps the person would need to follow, in order. Use the organizer below to plan your composition. Then write it on a separate sheet of paper.

How-to Topic: (Write a topic sentence that tells what skill you will be explaining.)	Materials or Equipment Needed:

Step 1:

(Remember to use time-order words such as *first*.)

Step 2:

(Use time-order words such as *next* and *then*.)

Step 3:

Step 4:

(Use time-order words such as *finally* or *last*.)

Harcourt Brace School Publishers

Name _____

Vocabulary and Concepts

ornaments
radial balance
patterns

A Complete each sentence with a word or phrase from the box.

1. A circular design that fans out from the center shows _____.

2. People use _____ to decorate a place.

3. Repeated shapes, colors, or lines are called _____.

B Use Drawings A and B to answer questions 4–5. Answer each question with a complete sentence.

Drawing A

Drawing B

4. Which shows something from nature, Drawing A, Drawing B, or both? Explain.

_____

_____

5. Which design has radial balance, Drawing A, Drawing B, or both? Explain.

_____

_____

6. Think about the ornaments shown in Lesson 22. How did the Native Americans of the southwestern plains use these ornaments?

_____

_____

7. What was the Plains Indians' symbol of how everything in the world is connected?

_____

Write a Friendly Letter

 Plan and Write   Write a friendly letter to a Plains Indian artist, such as the Arapaho or Sioux artist who made the ornaments in Lesson 22. Think about what you would like to tell the artist about yourself and what you want to know about him or her. Be sure to include the five parts of a friendly letter. Write your ideas clearly and in detail. Use the organizer below to plan your letter. Then write it on another piece of paper.

Greeting	**Heading**
Dear _____, Write a name for the artist here.	Your address: Today's date:

First paragraph: Introduce yourself to the artist. Tell where you live and where you go to school. Describe in detail how you have decorated a room at home or at school with things that are special to you.

Detail 1:

Detail 2:

Detail 3:

Second paragraph: Ask the artist some specific questions that you want answered about his or her life, such as what living on the southwestern plains is like or how he or she became an artist.

Question 1:

Question 2:

Question 3:

Last paragraph: Think of a way to end the letter.

Closing

Sincerely,

_____

Write your **signature** here.

(B O D Y of L E T T E R)

Name _____

Vocabulary and Concepts

A Label the drawings with words from the box. Then write a word from the box to complete the sentence.

1. _____   2. _____

3. The pictures show two styles of building design, or _____.

B Circle the letter next to the correct answer for questions 4–6. Write answers to question 7.

4. In which country were roofs that curve up at the ends first made?
   A. the United States   **B.** China   **C.** Spain

5. People from Spain brought which two designs to the United States?
   A. arches and dome-shaped roofs   **B.** dome-shaped roofs and pyramids
   C. pyramids and arches

6. Which statement about pyramid-shaped buildings is true?
   A. The pyramid shape is found in modern and ancient buildings.
   B. The pyramid shape is found only in modern buildings.
   C. The pyramid shape is found only in ancient buildings.

7. What architectural feature(s) made each building you studied in Lesson 23 distinctive?

   San José Mission: _____

   Japanese Tea House and Garden: _____

   Transamerica Tower: _____

Write About Likes and Dislikes

 Plan and Write   Lesson 23 shows three distinctive buildings. Think of a building in your community that is distinctive in some way. Write a composition for your teacher explaining both what you like about this building, both inside and out, and what you do not like about it. Be sure to explain your ideas in detail. Use the organizer below to plan your composition, and write it on a separate piece of paper.

First, name your topic. Write a catchy opening sentence.

Next, list three things you like about the building, such as how it looks outside, how it looks inside, or how it is used. Add a reason why you like each detail.

Detail 1:

Reason:

Detail 2:

Reason:

Detail 3:

Reason:

Now list three things you do not like. Again, include details and reasons.

Detail 1:

Reason:

Detail 2:

Reason:

Detail 3:

Reason:

Finally, write an ending that summarizes the good points and bad points.

Name _____

Vocabulary and Concepts

 A Label each drawing with a word or phrase from the box.

shadow puppet
puppets
marionette

1. _____ 2. _____ 3. _____

B For items 4–7, choose the best answer and fill in the circle of your choice. Write the answer to item 8.

ANSWERS

4. Ⓐ Ⓑ Ⓒ Ⓓ
5. Ⓐ Ⓑ Ⓒ Ⓓ
6. Ⓐ Ⓑ Ⓒ Ⓓ
7. Ⓐ Ⓑ Ⓒ Ⓓ

4. What helps a marionette move?

  A. a motor   **C.** its feet

  B. wheels   **D.** strings

5. What is in front of a shadow puppet during a show?

  A. a thin screen   **C.** a bright light

  B. a heavy curtain   **D.** the person operating the puppet

6. What do you see during a shadow puppet show?

  A. the shadow cast by the puppet   **C.** strings attached to the puppet

  B. the person operating the puppet   **D.** wires attached to the puppet

7. Where are the puppets you read about in Lesson 24 from?

  A. Japan and Africa   **C.** America and Egypt

  B. China and Austria   **D.** Japan and England

8. How are all puppets alike? _____

_____

Write a Puppet Story

 Plan and Write   Think of three puppet characters such as a young prince, a wise frog, and a powerful queen. Write a story about them. Use the story map below to plan your story. Then write it on a separate piece of paper.

Setting: (Describe where and when the story takes place.)	Characters: (Describe who the puppets are and what they are like.)

Problem:

IDEA BANK:

- outsmart a villain
- win a singing contest
- protect a castle from a dragon
- take a long journey

Beginning:

(Remember to use time-order words such as *first* or *one day*.)

Middle:

    Event 1:

    Event 2:

    Event 3:

(Use time-order words such as *then, later on,* and *next.*)

Solution:

(Think of a clever way for the puppets to solve the problem.)

End:

(Use time-order words such as *finally.*)

Name _____

A **Complete each sentence with an art term from the box.**

> architecture
> shadow puppet
> negative shapes
> kiln
> variety
> marionette

1. A _____ is a puppet moved by strings.

2. The design of buildings is called _____.

3. Artists use a _____ to bake clay objects.

4. A _____ is held behind a thin screen during a show.

5. A cut-paper figure has empty spaces, called _____, between and around other shapes.

6. A mask may have a _____ of textures, such as bumpy, smooth, and rough.

B **Circle the letter next to the word or phrase that best completes each sentence.**

7. The _____ lines in a drawing are lines you can see.
   A. negative   **B.** implied   **C.** actual

8. The _____ lines in a drawing are hidden.
   A. implied   **B.** actual   **C.** negative

9. Vessels and other objects made out of baked clay are called _____.
   A. ceremonial   **B.** ornaments   **C.** pottery

10. People use _____ to decorate the places they live.
    A. ornaments   **B.** radial balance   **C.** positive shapes

11. Each side of a _____ is in the shape of a triangle.
    A. kiln   **B.** pyramid   **C.** cube

C | **On a separate sheet of paper, draw answers to items 12 and 13. Write answers to items 14–20.**

12. Draw a simple picture of a mask.

13. Draw a simple ornament that shows radial balance.

14. Name two traditional art forms that are found in many cultures. _____

_____

15. For what purpose have people traditionally used puppets? _____

_____

16. Why is pottery called a *practical* art form? _____

_____

17. Is it true that architects often get ideas from the past? If your answer is yes, give an

example. _____

18. Name one symbol that comes from a Native American culture. Tell what the symbol

stands for. _____

19. Pottery is made in many cultures. How do potters make their work unique and

different from one another? _____

_____

20. Find an artwork displayed in your classroom that fits well in this unit, "Reflections."
Write the artwork's title and artist and explain why you chose it. _____

_____

_____

| **TEACHER NOTE** | **Display several *Art Prints* while students complete these pages.** |

Name _____

Vocabulary and Concepts

A Write the letter of each definition on the right on the line next to the word or phrase it matches.

1. **photography** _____   **A.** a view from the ground looking up

2. **worm's-eye** view _____   **B.** a view directly across from the viewer

3. **bird's-eye** view _____   **C.** the art of taking pictures

4. **eye level** view _____   **D.** a view from above looking down

B Circle the letter next to the correct answer.

5. Look at *Art Print 10, The Temple of Kukulcan.* From what point of view did the photographer take the picture of the temple?
   A. bird's-eye view   **B.** worm's-eye view   **C.** eye-level view

6. What point of view would you have if you looked at your school from an airplane?
   A. bird's-eye view   **B.** worm's-eye view   **C.** eye-level view

7. From a worm's-eye point of view, an object looks _____ than it does from an eye-level view.
   A. taller   **B.** smaller   **C.** duller

8. Why do photographers take pictures using different points of view?
   A. to make the pictures brighter and more colorful
   B. to make the pictures seem smaller
   C. to make the pictures more interesting and dramatic

TEACHER NOTE Display *Art Print 10* while students complete this page.

Write a Description

 Plan and Write   Imagine that you are the Statue of Liberty looking at New York City from the harbor. Write a descriptive paragraph for your teacher telling what you see. Be sure to include colorful details that give your reader a clear picture of what you see. Use the organizer below to plan your paragraph. Then write it on a separate sheet of paper.

First, write a sentence telling who you are and what your point of view of New York City is. (Remember to use *I* in your sentence.)

Next, write details about what you see. Use specific adjectives to make your writing more interesting. (When you write your paragraph, be sure to group details that belong together.)

What the buildings look like:
What the harbor and the boats look like:
What you hear:
How it feels to have tourists taking photographs of you:

Finally, write a conclusion that summarizes why your point of view is unusual.

Name _____

Vocabulary and Concepts

A Circle the letter next to the phrase that best completes each sentence.

1. The purpose of a **memorial** is to help us _____.
   A. celebrate holidays   B. honor our heroes   C. decorate our communities

2. A **maquette** is _____.
   A. any three-dimensional shape
   B. a detailed list of materials
   C. a miniature version of an artwork

3. A **scale model** is _____.
   A. larger than life-size   B. life-size   C. smaller than life-size

B Write an answer to each question below. Use complete sentences.

4. Do all memorials look alike? Explain. _____

   _____

5. Think about the huge memorial shown in Lesson 26 that was built to honor police

   officers. Describe its shape and size. _____

   _____

6. Think about the relief sculpture in Lesson 26 that shows different faces. Which group

   of people does that memorial honor? _____

   _____

7. How is a maquette useful in making large works of art such as memorials? _____

   _____

Name _____

Write a Friendly Letter

 Plan and Write   In Lesson 26 you read about memorials for heroes. Think of someone whom you consider a hero, and write a letter to that person. Be sure to include the five parts of a friendly letter. Write your ideas clearly and in detail. Use the organizer below to plan your letter. Then write it on another sheet of paper.

Greeting	**Heading**
Dear _____, (Write the hero's name here.)	Your address: Today's date:

First paragraph: Introduce yourself to the hero. Tell where you live, where you go to school, and what activities you enjoy.

Detail 1:

Detail 2:

Detail 3:

Second paragraph: Ask the hero some specific questions that about his or her life, such as what that person's job is like, what he or she does for fun, and what he or she thinks about being a hero.

Question 1:

Question 2:

Question 3:

Closing
Sincerely,

_____
(Write your **signature** here.)

B
O
D
Y

o
f

L
E
T
T
E
R

Harcourt Brace School Publishers

Name _____

Vocabulary and Concepts

message
mural
public

A Write each word from the box next to its meaning.

1. _____ a painting on a wall

2. _____ in view of the entire community

3. _____ an important idea communicated to others

B Write a complete sentence to answer items 4–6. Circle the letter next to the correct answer for item 7.

4. Why do people paint murals? _____

_____

5. Did the artists of the murals in Lesson 27 create the murals alone? Explain your

answer. _____

_____

6. The students who created the Houston mural included flags from many countries in the artwork. What message do you think the artists wanted to communicate?

_____

_____

7. What message did the artist of *The Great Wall of Los Angeles* want to give through her mural?
   A. People should do volunteer work in the community.
   B. People of different backgrounds are valuable to the community.
   C. People should recycle in order to protect the environment.

Write to Persuade

 Plan and Write Lesson 27 showed two murals that mean a lot to their communities. Write an essay trying to convince your principal that a mural should be painted on one of your school's walls. Include what the mural will look like, its message, and reasons why it should be painted. Use the organizer below to plan your composition, and write it on another sheet of paper.

Write the beginning.

Opinion statement:

Write the middle. Briefly describe the mural and its message. Write three reasons to support your opinion that a mural should be painted. For each reason, give at least one fact or emotional appeal. Put the most important reason first.

Reason 1: Fact:
Reason 2: Fact:
Reason 3: Fact:

Write your conclusion. State your opinion in different words. Then tell what your principal should do.

Harcourt Brace School Publishers

Name _____

Vocabulary and Concepts

symmetrical balance
landscaped
asymmetrical balance

A Use a word or phrase from the box to complete each sentence.

Drawing A

Drawing B

1. The garden in **A** has _____.

2. The garden in **B** has _____.

3. A _____ garden has been carefully designed and cared for.

B Circle the letter next to the correct answer for questions 4 and 5. Write complete sentences to answer questions 6 and 7.

4. What is a landscaped garden with *symmetrical balance* like?
   A. It has only one type of plant in it.
   B. The plants are grouped in a varied pattern.
   C. Each side is a mirror image of the other side.

5. What is a landscaped garden with *asymmetrical balance* like?
   A. It is unplanned and not well cared for.
   B. The plants are grouped in a varied pattern.
   C. It is grown only in Japan.

6. What things might you see in a landscaped garden? _____

   _____

7. Why are landscaped gardens sometimes called works of art? _____

   _____

Write a How-to Paragraph

▶ **Plan and Write** Gardeners must take many steps to keep their gardens healthy and beautiful. Write a how-to paragraph explaining to a friend how to plant a seed in order to grow a house plant or garden plant. List the steps your friend would need to follow. Be sure to explain them in order. You can use the pictures below to help you. Use the organizer to plan your composition. Then write it on a separate sheet of paper.

How-to Topic:	Materials or Equipment Needed:

Step 1:

Step 2:

Step 3:

Step 4:

Harcourt Brace School Publishers

Name _____

Vocabulary and Concepts

mosque
cathedral
minarets

A Label the drawings with words from the box.

1. _____ 2. _____ 3. _____

B Answer the following items using complete sentences.

4. Look at *Art Print 10, The Temple of Kukulcan.* How is this building like the buildings

you studied in Lesson 29? _____

_____

5. Why are historical buildings very special to the countries they are in?

_____

_____

6. Describe the shape of a mosque's roof. Describe another special feature many mosques

have. _____

_____

7. Do you think the architects who designed the cathedral and the mosque shown in
Lesson 29 expected these buildings to last for a long time? Explain your answer.

_____

_____

TEACHER NOTE Display *Art Print 10* while students complete this page.

Write a Story

 Plan and Write   In Lesson 29 you saw two historical buildings. Imagine that you and a friend are exploring in an old building at night and you come upon a hidden door. Write a story about what happens when you open the door. Include colorful details to make your story interesting. Tell the story events in order, using time-order words. Use the story map below to plan your story. Then write it on another sheet of paper.

Setting:	Characters:

Problem:

IDEA BANK:

- meet an artist
- find a strange object
- discover a secret
- find a tunnel or maze

Beginning:

Middle:
Event 1:
Event 2:
Event 3:

Solution:

End:

Name _____

Vocabulary and Concepts

| translucent |
| lead |
| stained-glass |

A Write a word from the box that best completes each sentence.

A **1.** ___ window is made of pieces of colored glass arranged in a design. The glass is **2.** ___, which means that light can pass through it. Glassmakers use **3.** ___, a kind of soft metal, to hold the small pieces of glass in place.

1. _____   2. _____   3. _____

B Choose the best answer and fill in the circle of your choice.

ANSWERS
4. (A) (B) (C) (D)
5. (A) (B) (C) (D)
6. (A) (B) (C) (D)
7. (A) (B) (C) (D)

4. The stained-glass window of Notre Dame Cathedral is called a *rose window* because it _____.
   A. has a soft pink color   C. is made of colored glass
   B. looks out onto a garden   D. has a flowerlike shape

5. What did glassmakers of the Middle Ages add to melted glass to create different colors?
   A. crushed berries and plants   B. dyes   C. metals   D. paints

6. What part of the stained-glass window of Notre Dame shows *radial balance?*
   A. the thick lines fanning from the center
   B. the light shining through the glass
   C. the small pieces of lead between each small piece of glass
   D. the people pictured in the window

7. Which statement about the stained-glass window of Notre Dame is correct?
   A. It is formed out of a few large pieces of glass.
   B. It is formed out of thousands of pieces of glass.
   C. It lets viewers clearly see things outside the cathedral.
   D. It blocks light from inside the cathedral.

Write About Likes and Dislikes

 Plan and Write   Imagine you lived long ago, in the days before electricity, supermarkets, and other modern conveniences. Pick a period such as Colonial times, Wild West days, or another time in the past. Write a composition for your teacher explaining both what you would like about living in that time and what you would not like about it. Explain your ideas in detail. Use the organizer below to plan your composition, and write it on a separate sheet of paper.

First, name your topic. Write a catchy opening sentence.

Next, list three things you would like about living long ago. Add a reason for each detail.

Detail 1:

Reason:

Detail 2:

Reason:

Detail 3:

Reason:

Now list three things you would not like. Again, add details and reasons.

Detail 1:

Reason:

Detail 2:

Reason:

Detail 3:

Reason:

Finally, write an ending that summarizes the good points and bad points.

Name _____

A Write the letter of each definition next to the word it matches.

1. mural   _____   **A.** letting light pass through

2. maquette   _____   **B.** a large Christian church

3. cathedral   _____   **C.** for the use of everyone in a community

4. translucent _____   **D.** a small model used to plan a memorial

5. public   _____   **E.** a painting on a wall

B Circle the letter next to the word or phrase that best completes each sentence.

6. The artist's _____ view of the redwood tree made it look even taller than it actually was.
   A. worm's-eye   **B.** eye-level   **C.** bird's-eye   **D.** Surrealist

7. Many _____ have been built in Washington, D.C., to help us honor and remember national heroes.
   A. maquettes   **B.** memorials **C.** mosques   **D.** cathedrals

8. The design of a _____ typically includes one or more domes and tall towers called minarets.
   A. mosque   **B.** memorial **C.** mural   **D.** cathedral

9. A _____ window is made of colored pieces of glass held together by lead.
   A. dyed   **B.** mosque   **C.** minaret   **D.** stained-glass

10. A picture with _____ is one that has different images on either side of a center line.
   A. symmetrical balance **B.** proportion **C.** point of view   **D.** asymmetrical balance

C On a separate sheet of paper, draw answers to items 11 and 12. Write answers to items 13–20.

11. Draw a simple design with **symmetrical balance.**

12. Draw a sketch showing a **bird's-eye view** of the street you live on.

13. How can a photographer make a photograph look more interesting and dramatic?

_____

14. Why do people build memorials in their communities? _____

_____

15. Name two forms of public art shown in this unit. _____

_____

16. What can murals show about the people in a community? Give one example to

support your answer. _____

_____

17. Do all landscaped gardens have symmetrical balance? Explain. _____

_____

18. Both mosques and cathedrals are used for _____.

19. Describe the process of making stained-glass windows. _____

_____

20. Find an artwork displayed in your classroom that fits well in this unit, "Inspirations." Write the artwork's title and artist and explain why you chose it.

_____

_____

Harcourt Brace School Publishers

TEACHER NOTE Display several Art Prints while students complete this page.

Name _____

Vocabulary and Concepts

Surrealist
unexpected
impossible

 A Match each word in the box with its meaning. Write the words on the lines.

1. art that shows dreamlike images in a reasonable way _____

2. something that could not happen in real life _____

3. something that is surprising _____

B Circle the letter next to the best answer for questions 4 and 5. Write the answers to items 6–8.

4. Why does Salvador Dalí's painting of the watches in Lesson 31 look unreal?
   A. The watches are bent like cloth.
   B. The ground is full of shadows.
   C. The sky is too dark.

5. What is the strangest part of René Magritte's painting of men in Lesson 31?
   A. The buildings are painted unusual colors.
   B. The men are standing in the air.
   C. The men are wearing costumes and masks.

6. Look at *Art Print 12, The Persistence of Memory*. Which parts of the painting look realistic? _____

   _____

7. What is dreamlike about the painting? _____

   _____

8. Is the painting an example of Surrealist art? Why or why not? _____

   _____

TEACHER NOTE | Display *Art Print 12* while students complete this page.

Harcourt Brace School Publishers

Name _____

Write a Fantasy Story

 Plan and Write   One of the paintings in Lesson 31 shows people who float in the air. Imagine that you wake up one morning with the ability to fly. Write a fantasy story about what happens. Be sure to describe or make clear the setting, the characters, the story problem, the main events, the solution, and an ending. Use the story map below to plan your fantasy story, and write it on a separate piece of paper.

Setting:	Characters:

Problem:

IDEA BANK

• catch an escaped parakeet

• smash a dangerous meteor into tiny pieces

• collect clouds to end a drought

• save a parachuter

Beginning:

Middle:

Solution:

End:

Name _____

Vocabulary and Concepts

pulp
canvas
continuous
dyed

A Match each word in the box with its meaning.
Write the words on the lines.

1. special thick cloth artists paint on _____

2. changed the color of something using colored liquid _____

3. the liquid form of paper _____

4. moving in an endless way _____

B To answer item 5, circle the letter next to the right answer. For items 6 and 7,
write the answers on the lines.

5. What is the main idea of Lesson 32?
   A. Artists often follow the traditions of the past when they make art.
   B. Jackson Pollock and David Hockney have similar styles.
   C. Artists sometimes use new materials and methods when they make art.
   D. Paper pulp can be used to make a picture of a pool.

6. David Hockney created texture in his picture of a pool by _____

   _____.

7. Jackson Pollock created texture in his painting by _____

   _____.

Harcourt Brace School Publishers

Lesson 32

CREATING IN UNUSUAL WAYS

Write a Comparison

> **Plan and Write** Lesson 32 shows a painting of a swimming pool. Write a composition for your teacher comparing two bodies of water, such as a swimming pool and a lake, river, or ocean. In the first paragraph, tell how the bodies of water are alike. In the second paragraph, tell how they are different. Be sure to include plenty of details in your comparison. Use the chart below to plan your composition. Write your composition on another piece of paper.

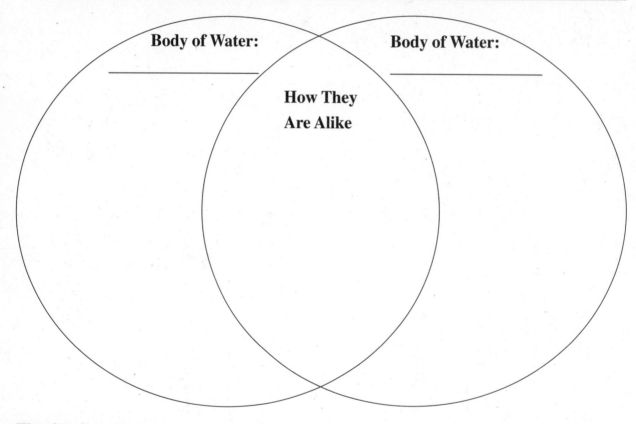

Body of Water: _____

Body of Water: _____

How They Are Alike

Tips for Comparing

1. Begin the first paragraph with a topic sentence that tells what you are comparing. Give two or three details that tell how the two bodies of water are alike. (Use signal words such as *both.*)

2. Begin the second paragraph with a topic sentence, too. Then give two or three details that tell how the two bodies of water are different.

3. In the last sentence, tell which body of water you like better, and why.

Informative Writing

Harcourt Brace School Publishers

Name _____

Vocabulary and Concepts

| balanced |
| arranged |
| mobiles |

A Complete each sentence with a word from the box.

1. Moveable sculptures are called _____.

2. The shapes can be _____ in a pattern of colors.

3. The shapes must be _____ so the sculpture will not tip over and so that its parts can move freely.

B Choose the best answer for each item and fill in the circle of your choice.

4. Mobiles are different from other types of sculptures because mobiles _____.
   A. have hanging parts that move
   B. have interesting shapes
   C. are three-dimensional
   D. look exactly like real objects

ANSWERS

4. (A) (B) (C) (D)
5. (A) (B) (C) (D)
6. (A) (B) (C) (D)
7. (A) (B) (C) (D)

5. To make a mobile, artist Alexander Calder *first* _____.
   A. placed the shapes in patterns
   B. cut out hundreds of shapes
   C. attached the shapes to the stand
   D. built a sturdy stand

6. Both of the mobiles in Lesson 33 _____.
   A. hang from the ceiling
   B. are attached to a frame on the ground
   C. show the same objects
   D. are carefully balanced

7. How is a mobile like a seesaw?
   A. Both have the same shape.
   B. Both are found in playgrounds.
   C. Both must be balanced in order to move.
   D. Both must be made of metal and wood.

Write About a Personal Mobile

 Plan and Write   Lesson 33 showed a mobile of important objects in a fisher's life, including a lobster trap and a fish. Suppose you wanted to make a mobile in which the moveable parts are objects important in your life. What objects would you choose? Write a letter to your teacher about your personal mobile. Tell what objects will be part of your mobile and why you have chosen each one. Use the organizer below to plan your letter, and write it on a separate sheet of paper.

Greeting Dear _____, (Write your teacher's name here.)	**Heading** Your address: Today's date:	
Introductory sentence:		
What objects will be portrayed in the mobile Object 1:	**Why I have included it**	B O D Y o f L E T T E R
Object 2:		
Object 3:		
Object 4:		
Last paragraph: Think of a way to end your letter.		
Closing Your student, _____ Write your signature here.		

Name _____

Vocabulary and Concepts

represent
nonrepresentational
curving

A Write a word from the box to complete each sentence about the drawings below.

Drawing 1

Drawing 2

1. The sculpture in **Drawing 1** is _____. It is not supposed to look like anything else.

2. The sculptures in **Drawing 2** _____, or look like, whales.

3. The two sculptures have _____, or rounded, shapes.

B Write an answer to each question below. Use complete sentences.

4. Think about the sculptures in Lesson 34: *Texas Shield* and *Hollow Form with White Interior.* How are these two sculptures alike?_____

_____

5. Look at *Art Print 5, Sodbuster: San Isidro.* Is this a nonrepresentational sculpture? Why or why not?_____

_____

6. Look at *Art Print 11, Lever No. 3.* How is this sculpture like the two sculptures shown in Lesson 34?_____

_____

TEACHER NOTE Display *Art Prints 5* and *11* while students complete this page.

Write to Compare and Contrast

Plan and Write   One sculpture in lesson 34 was made of wood, and one was made of stone. Write a composition comparing wood and stone—two of the most useful and plentiful materials in the world. Use the organizer below to help you plan your paragraphs, and write them on another sheet of paper.

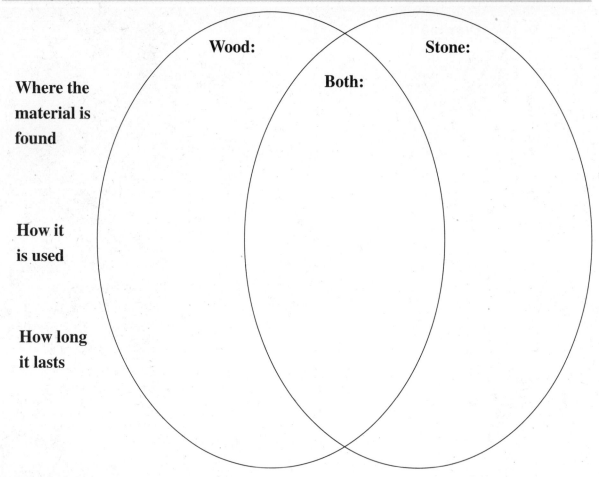

Where the material is found

How it is used

How long it lasts

Wood:

Both:

Stone:

Tips for Comparing

1. Begin the first paragraph with a topic sentence that tells what you are comparing. Give two or three details that tell how the two materials are alike.

2. Begin the second paragraph with a topic sentence, too. Then give two or three details that tell how the two materials are different.

3. Use signal words such as *both* and *neither*.

4. Begin the third paragraph with a sentence that tells which material you like better, and why.

Harcourt Brace School Publishers

Name _____

Vocabulary and Concepts

A Write the letter of each word on the right in the blank where it belongs.

1. Something that is _____ is strong and reliable.   **A. whimsical**

2. Artworks can be made out of many different _____ .   **B. sturdy**

3. A person who creates sculptures is called a _____.   **C. sculptor**

4. Something that is _____ is fanciful or playful.   **D. materials**

B Circle the letter next to the correct answer in items 5 and 6. Write the answer to item 7.

5. Which statement is true about sculptors?
   A. Sculptors always know what they are going to make before they select their material.
   B. Sometimes sculptors get an idea from the materials themselves.
   C. Sculptors never know what they are going to make before they begin a sculpture.

6. Remember the sculpture called *Working Woman* from Lesson 35. What idea does it seem to express?
   A. It takes strength to balance work and family.
   B. Women are stronger than men.
   C. It is easy to be a working mother.

7. Look at *Art Print 5, Sodbuster: San Isidro* and *Art Print 11, Lever No. 3.* Which

   sculpture looks more whimsical? Why? _____

   _____

| **TEACHER NOTE** | Display *Art Prints 5* and *11* while students complete this page. |

Harcourt Brace School Publishers

Write a How-to Paragraph

 Plan and Write   One of the sculptures in Lesson 35 shows a woman who looks like she is getting ready to go to work. Suppose you want to explain to a younger relative or friend how to get ready for school, a field trip, a sport, or a camping trip. Choose an outing that a person must prepare for. Be sure to discuss the steps in order. Use the organizer below to plan your composition, and write it on a separate sheet of paper.

How-to Topic: (Write a topic sentence that tells what you will be explaining.)	**Materials or Belongings Needed:**

Step 1:

(Remember to use time-order words such as *first*.)

Step 2:

(Use time-order words such as *next* and *then*.)

Step 3:

Step 4:

(Use time-order words such as *finally* or *last*.)

Name _____

Vocabulary and Concepts

| illusion |
| height |
| architect |

A Complete each sentence with a word from the box.

1. An _____ is someone who designs buildings.

2. The _____ of a building is how tall it is.

3. An _____ tricks the eye because it looks real but isn't.

B Write a phrase to complete item 4. Use the picture to answer items 5–7.

4. Think of the picture *Waterfall* by M. C. Escher shown in Lesson 36. The flow of water

   does not make sense because _____

   _____.

5. Which line looks

   longer, A or B?

   _____

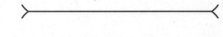

Line A

Line B

6. Now measure the horizontal (flat) part of each line. How do their lengths compare?

   _____

   _____

7. Why is the picture of lines an *illusion*? _____

   _____

TEACHER NOTE Provide students with rulers while they complete this page.

Write a Story

> **Plan and Write**   Imagine that you have entered a world where water flows uphill and plants are as big as people. Write a story for your teacher about an adventure you have in this unusual world. Remember to refer to yourself as *I*. Use the organizer below to make notes for your narrative. Then write it on a separate sheet of paper.

Beginning

First, tell where you went and who you went with. Write an opening sentence that grabs the reader's attention. Include details that will help your readers visualize the place.

Middle

Next, list the events that happened in the order they occurred. Include a detailed description of each event. Also describe how you and others felt during the experience.

Event 1:

    Description/Details:

Event 2:

    Description/Details:

Event 3:

    Description/Details:

Ending

Finally, write a conclusion that tells how the experience ended. Summarize the reasons why this experience was special for you.

Name _____

A **Write the word from the box that goes with each definition below.**

| whimsical |
| mobiles |
| represent |
| Surrealist |
| unexpected |
| pulp |

1. showing dreamlike images in a

   realistic way _____

2. fanciful or playful _____

3. liquid form of paper _____

4. sculptures that move _____

5. surprising _____

6. look like _____

B **Circle the letter next to the best answer.**

7. a thick cloth artists paint on

   A. pulp   **B.** frame   **C.** canvas

8. artwork that is not meant to look like anything

   A. Surrealist   **B.** nonrepresentational   **C.** whimsical

9. a person who makes sculptures

   A. sculptor   **B.** architect   **C.** photographer

10. something that tricks the eye

    A. illusion   **B.** mobile   **C.** asymmetrical balance

11. a person who designs buildings

    A. sculptor   **B.** architect   **C.** photographer

C Circle the letter to answer items 11–14. Write the answers to items 15–20.

12. To move, a mobile needs to _____.
    A. be properly balanced   B. have a motor   C. be put on wheels

13. To make his picture of a pool, David Hockney used _____.
    A. pen and ink   B. foil and spattered paint   C. molded paper pulp

14. M.C. Escher is known for drawings _____.
    A. of abstract figures   B. of animals   C. that trick the eye

15. The picture *Waterfall* by M.C. Escher was impossible because it showed _____.
    A. nonrepresentational designs   B. water flowing uphill   C. flying people

16. Sometimes artists experiment with new methods and materials. Give one example of

    this kind of experimentation from Unit 6. _____

    _____

17. Look at *Art Print 2, Still Life.* Is this a Surrealist painting? Why or why not? _____

    _____

18. What unusual technique did Jackson Pollock use to show texture in his paintings?

    _____

19. How can artists surprise viewers with their artwork? Give one example from Unit 6.

    _____

20. Find an artwork displayed in your classroom that fits well in this unit "Expect the
    Unexpected." Write the artwork's title and artist and explain why you chose it.

    _____

    _____

TEACHER NOTE   Display *Art Prints 2, 3, 6* and *9* while students complete this page.

Unit 1

Lesson 1   Rock Art Pages 3–4

1. carved
2. petroglyphs
3. outline
4. A
5. C
6. C
7. A
8. Responses will vary. Students might mention the ox's sharp horns, long nose, large eyes, bulky body, and sturdy legs.

Lesson 2   Artful Regions Pages 5–6

1. background
2. middle ground
3. foreground
4. landscapes
5. Possible response: sand, cacti, the sun, desert animals such as snakes and lizards
6. Possible response: Artists make some objects look bigger in order to make them seem closer than others.
7. Possible response: Artists place some objects in the foreground of a painting to make them seem closer than others.

Lesson 3   An Artist's Favorite Mountain Pages 7–8

1. point of view
2. shape
3. proportion
4. The artist's point of view is from behind the man rowing the boat.
5. Possible responses: The artist used a triangle for the sail, circles or ovals for the people's hats and faces, and rectangles for the oars, houses, and slats in the boat.
6. The artist made the houses look far away by making them very small.
7. The man is larger in proportion to the woman.

Lesson 4   Nature's Shapes Pages 9–10

1. A
2. B
3. C
4. You can see more details in a close-up view.

5. Yes. Its star shape is rounded and uneven; the shape is found in nature.
6. Possible response: I could paint some starfish a darker color brown and others a lighter color brown so that they would stand out more.

Lesson 5   Natural Scenes Pages 11–12

1. B
2. D
3. A
4. C
5. They often show the animal's natural environment.
6. The artist of the deer showed the deer in a mountain setting. The artist of the bird showed the bird in its home in a tree.
7. Possible response: I would paint the sea and some icebergs in the background. I would put figures of a mother seal and some baby seals in the foreground.
8. Possible response: The background in the polar bear painting would probably show a white, frozen land. The background in the picture of the monkey would probably show lots of leafy green trees.

Lesson 6   Still Lifes Pages 13–14

1. still life
2. overlap
3. center of interest
4. A
5. B
6. A
7. C

Unit 1 Review   Beauty All Around Pages 15–16

1. B
2. C
3. A
4. B
5. A
6. C
7. A
8. B
9. D
10. E
11. Possible response: They drew or carved figures on rocks and cave walls.

Harcourt Brace School Publishers

12. Drawings will vary. Students should include a simple outline of the shell, head, and legs.

13.–14. A gargoyle is in the foreground; city buildings are in the background.

15.–16. Drawings will vary. Students should show an object from two different points of view.

17. the vase

18. Possible response: the shapes of the vase, flower, fruit, shells

19. Possible response: Placement—the artist placed some items lower to make them look closer to the viewer.

20. Responses will vary.

Unit 2

Lesson 7   Portraits Pages 17–18

1. C
2. B
3. A
4. Artists create portraits to show how people look or to show what people are like.
5. Possible response: You can see when and where the person lived, how old the person was, and maybe what that person did for a living.
6. Artists use proportion to help them make a person's features the right size.

Lesson 8   Relief Sculptures Pages 19–20

1. relief sculpture
2. profile
3. texture
4. True.
5. False. They can be any size from huge to tiny.
6. False. Relief sculptures are raised up from the background they are carved on.
7. True.

Lesson 9   Abstract Portraits Pages 21–22

1. abstract
2. triangle
3. cube
4. model
5. Possible response: The original painting showed how the princess really looked, and

Picasso's portrait experimented with shapes and colors.

6. Both pictures show the same girl.

7. Possible responses (any two): Picasso used triangles, circles, cubes, rectangles, and ovals.

8. A

Lesson 10   Shades and Tints Pages 23–24

1. monochromatic
2. shades
3. tints
4. mood
5. Possible response: *Poor People on the Seashore (The Tragedy)* has mostly cool blue tones, while *El Pan Nuestro* has warm tones of red, orange, and brown. The mood of Picasso's painting is sad, while the mood of Rivera's painting is cheerful.
6. Yes, because the main color is blue; all the colors have the same tone.
7. cool
8. mood

Lesson 11   Rhythm and Unity Pages 25–26

1. A
2. C
3. B
4. The clock image is repeated three times.
5. The artist used blues and oranges to create unity in the painting.
6. The colors black and orange are repeated in different parts of the design.

Lesson 12   People in Motion Pages 27–28

1. horizontal line
2. diagonal line
3. movement
4. False. Action lines can be horizontal or diagonal.
5. True.
6. True.
7. False. The oar and the sail are in a diagonal position and suggest movement.

Unit 2 Review   Picturing People Pages 29–30

1. B
2. E
3. A

4. D
5. C
6. C
7. C
8. A
9. A
10. B
11. Drawings will vary. Students should include a profile of a person's head.
12. Drawings will vary. Students should draw a figure in a moving position and include horizontal or diagonal lines to emphasize the movement.
13. An artist might create a portrait or a relief sculpture to show what a person looks like. (Accept only one.)
14. An abstract portrait experiments with shapes and colors and does not show the person as he or she really looks. A realistic portrait shows a person as he or she looks in real life.
15. Artists can use warm colors like red or yellow to create a happy mood.
16. Possible responses (any three): circle, oval, rectangle, triangle, line
17. Possible responses (accept any one object and its values): Nuts, bread, and the top cheese have light and dark browns; bottom cheese has light and dark oranges; bottom tablecloth has light and dark rusts; top tablecloth has light and dark tans; grapes have light and dark greens and purples; apples have light and dark golds or reds; dishes and glass have light and dark grays.
18. The artist created unity by repeating the shapes and colors in his painting.
19. Possible response: There are diagonal lines showing movement in the shape of the man's body; the back, legs, and heads of the oxen; and the handles of the plow.
20. Responses will vary.

Unit 3

Lesson 13   Animal Sculptures Pages 31–32
1. three-dimensional
2. sculptures
3. still
4. C
5. A

6. The man and the oxen are not flat. The figures look like they can be viewed from many sides.
7. The oxen seem to be in motion. Their legs are bent and they seem to be plowing a field.

Lesson 14   Comic Strips Pages 33–34
1. Comic strips
2. cartoonist
3. characters
4. frame
5. The cartoonist can draw different kinds of lines on the character's face to show how the character is feeling.
6. The cartoonist can draw action lines outside the character.
7. No. Some comic strips have a message.
8. Possible responses: Don't compare yourself to others; be happy with who you are.

Lesson 15   Important Symbols Pages 35–36
1. coat of arms
2. state seal
3. symbol
4. B
5. C
6. C
7. A

Lesson 16   Common Products as Art Pages 37–38
1. Pop Art
2. print
3. stamp
4. B
5. A
6. B
7. This is an example of Pop Art because it shows everyday things (desserts) as works of art.

Lesson 17   Cityscapes Pages 39–40
1. cityscape
2. glow
3. scene
4. *Art Print 9, Gargoyle,* shows a cityscape.
5. C
6. I would expect to see more geometric shapes because many things found in cities, such as buildings, have geometric shapes.

7. Possible responses: Day scene: The light would probably come from the sun. Night scene: The light would probably come from the moon, from inside the buildings, and from streetlights.

Lesson 18   Artistic Styles Pages 41–42

1. B
2. D
3. C
4. A
5. The paintings are alike because all show trains. They are different because each train is done in a different style.
6. The painting is realistic because it includes details and shows what objects look like in real life.
7. Possible response: I think if this picture were done in a realistic style it would have more details, and the things in it would look more like they do in real life.
8. Possible response: It would have simple shapes and bright colors and would not include many details.

Unit 3 Review   Expressions Pages 43–44

1. D
2. D
3. A
4. B
5. C
6. stamp
7. three-dimensional
8. cityscape
9. print
10. comic strip
11. Pop Art
12. Drawings will vary. Students should include a shield shape with some design on it.
13. a sculpture
14. by drawing lines around a character or object
15. Possible response: They both have symbols that stand for important ideas.
16. Possible response: The clocks are probably symbols of time.
17. Artists can show different feelings about a subject by painting in different styles.
18. Both paintings show pictures of food. *Art Print 2* is realistic because it shows the food as it

actually looks. *Art Print 6* is a work of Pop Art. It shows food in a new and unusual way.
19. Possible response: An artist can paint a soft glow that makes the place look warm and friendly or he/she can use little light to make the mood sad and lonely.
20. Responses will vary.

Unit 4

Lesson 19   Marvelous Masks Pages 45–46

1. D
2. A
3. C
4. B
5. A
6. D
7. D
8. C

Lesson 20   Paper Shapes Pages 47–48

1. negative shapes
2. Implied
3. actual
4. Positive shapes
5. The elephant's ear is shown using a negative shape.
6. The blanket on the elephant's back is shown using negative shapes.
7. Possible response: I see implied lines, because where the elephant's feet touch the ground there are no actual lines.

Lesson 21   Pottery Pages 49–50

1. vessels
2. pottery
3. potter
4. kiln
5. False. Possible response: Pottery is found in museums, in homes, and in stores.
6. True.
7. False. Possible response: Pottery is often used in everyday life, for serving food, holding plants, and decorating homes.
8. True.

Lesson 22   Radial Balance Pages 51–52

1. radial balance
2. ornaments

3. patterns
4. Drawing B shows a flower, which is found in nature.
5. Both have radial balance because they have circular designs arranged around a center.
6. Native Americans of the southwestern plains used the ornaments to decorate their teepees.
7. The circle was a symbol of how everything in the world is connected.

Lesson 23   Styles of Architecture Pages 53–54

1. arches
2. pyramid
3. architecture
4. B
5. A
6. A
7. Possible response: The San José Mission has arches and domes. The Japanese Tea House has a Chinese-style roof that curves up at the ends. The Transamerica Tower is a skyscraper shaped like a pyramid.

Lesson 24   Puppets Pages 55–56

1. marionette
2. shadow puppet
3. puppets
4. D
5. A
6. A
7. B
8. Possible responses: All puppets can move; all puppets can be used to tell stories.

Unit 4 Review   Reflections Pages 57–58

1. marionette
2. architecture
3. kiln
4. shadow puppet
5. negative shapes
6. variety
7. C
8. A
9. C
10. A
11. B
12. Drawings will vary.
13. Drawings will vary.

14. Possible responses (any two): masks, cut-paper shapes, pottery, ornaments, puppets.
15. Both have been used by people to tell stories.
16. Possible response: Pottery is called a practical art form because pottery is both beautiful and useful.
17. Possible response: Yes. One example is the Japanese Tea House, which resembles Chinese architecture. OR One example is an American church that has domes and arches like the buildings of Spain. OR One example is a skyscraper that looks like a pyramid.
18. Possible responses (accept either one): The circle stands for how all things are connected; the bear paw stands for water.
19. Possible response: Potters from different cultures use different methods. They also use different colors, designs, and symbols.
20. Responses will vary.

Unit 5

Lesson 25   Photographic Point of View Pages 59–60

1. C
2. A
3. D
4. B
5. C
6. A
7. A
8. C

Lesson 26   Memorials for Heroes Pages 61–62

1. B
2. C
3. C
4. No. Some can be much larger than others, some are built in the ground, and some are relief sculptures of real people.
5. The memorial is in the shape of a pyramid. It is as big as a football field.
6. The memorial honors African American soldiers who fought in the Civil War.
7. It helps an artist plan what the memorial will look like before building it.

Lesson 27   Murals Pages 63–64

1. mural
2. public

3. message
4. Possible response: People paint murals to tell a story or to share a message.
5. Possible response: No. Many people in the community worked together to create the murals.
6. Possible response: They wanted to show that people from around the world live in their community; they wanted to celebrate diversity.
7. B

Lesson 28   Landscaped Gardens Pages 65–66

1. asymmetrical balance
2. symmetrical balance
3. landscaped
4. C
5. B
6. Possible response: I would see grass, trees, plants, rocks, and pools, all carefully arranged.
7. Possible responses: They show the beauty of plants and other objects; they are created for the enjoyment of others.

Lesson 29   Historical Buildings Pages 67–68

1. mosque
2. minarets
3. cathedral
4. Possible responses: It is a historical building; it was built as a place of worship.
5. Possible response: Historical buildings tell us about the traditions of the past.
6. Possible response: A mosque has a rounded, dome-shaped roof. Many mosques also have minarets, tall towers that are pointed at the top.
7. Possible response: Yes. The architects planned huge, important buildings that took a long time to build, so they must have expected them to last for many years.

Lesson 30   Stained-Glass Windows Pages 69–70

1. stained-glass
2. translucent
3. lead
4. D
5. C
6. A
7. B

Unit 5 Review   Inspirations Pages 71–72

1. E
2. D
3. B
4. A
5. C
6. A
7. B
8. A
9. D
10. D
11. Drawings will vary.
12. Drawings will vary.
13. Possible responses: A photographer can take a picture from a different point of view; a photographer can use contrast.
14. They build memorials to honor and remember heroes and other important people.
15. Possible responses (accept any two): memorials, murals, landscaped gardens, historical buildings
16. Possible responses: Murals can reflect who lives in a communty; they can tell about the contributions people or groups have made; they can tell a story; they can tell about a group's way of life. (Students' responses should include an example of a mural they have studied.)
17. Possible response: No. Landscaped gardens are any gardens that are carefully designed and cared for. They can have symmetrical balance or asymmetrical balance.
18. worship
19. Possible response: Artists make designs out of many pieces of colored glass and use strips of lead to hold the pieces together.
20. Responses will vary.

Unit 6

Lesson 31   Surrealist Art Pages 73–74

1. Surrealist
2. impossible
3. unexpected
4. A
5. B
6. The ocean, the cliffs, and the sky look realistic.
7. The watches look melted, a tree is growing

out of a block, and there is a strange creature lying on the ground.

8. Yes. Like other Surrealist paintings, this one shows unreal ideas in a reasonable way.

Lesson 32   Creating in Unusual Ways
Pages 75–76

1. canvas
2. dyed
3. pulp
4. continuous
5. C
6. molding paper pulp with combs, brushes, and other household objects
7. layering many lines of paint in long, looping trails

Lesson 33   A Balancing Act Pages 77–78

1. mobiles
2. arranged
3. balanced
4. A
5. B
6. D
7. C

Lesson 34   Unusual Forms Pages 79–80

1. nonrepresentational
2. represent
3. curving
4. The sculptures are alike in that both are nonrepresentational.
5. No. It isn't nonrepresentational because it's made to look like a man with his two oxen.
6. Its shape does not represent anything in real life.

Lesson 35   Whimsical Sculpture Pages 81–82

1. B
2. D
3. C
4. A
5. B
6. A
7. Possible response: *Lever No. 3* looks more whimsical, because the thin curling shape is playful.

Lesson 36   An Impossible Building Pages 83–84

1. architect
2. height
3. illusion
4. the water looks like it is flowing uphill
5. Students will probably write the Line B is longer.
6. They are the same length.
7. The picture is an illusion because it tricks the eye.

Unit 6 Review   Expect the Unexpected
Pages 85–86

1. Surrealist
2. whimsical
3. pulp
4. mobiles
5. unexpected
6. represent
7. C
8. B
9. A
10. A
11. B
12. A
13. C
14. C
15. B
16. Possible responses: Jackson Pollock dripped paint onto canvas to create an unusual effect; David Hockney experimented with paper pulp; Alexander Calder made sculptural mobiles. (Accept all other reasonable responses.)
17. No. A Surrealist painting would show dreamlike images in a realistic way. This picture shows life-like images.
18. He dripped and spattered paint on canvas.
19. Possible responses: (Accept any one) Artists can create Surrealist paintings that surprise viewers by showing possible objects in impossible ways; Artists can surprise people by using unusual materials as David Hockney did; They can surprise people by using unusual methods, as Jackson Pollock did; They can create sculptures with unusual shapes.
20. Responses will vary.

Student _____ Date _____
Evaluator _____

Rubric for Expressive Writing

The score of this composition is _____.
The composition has all or most of the characteristics listed in the chart below.

Score	Description
4 (high)	• The response is consistent and organized, giving the reader a sense of order and completeness. It tells a story from beginning to end, with a clear sense of time and place, by presenting and then resolving a problem. Any minor organizational inconsistencies are offset by the overall quality of the response. • The response includes clear, relevant, well-explained descriptions and rich, elaborated details that help the reader visualize story events. It contains a variety of sentence constructions and vivid words and phrases. • The response shows excellent control of language. Most conventions of spelling, grammar, usage, and punctuation are followed.
3	• The response is a good attempt to tell a story in a logical, sequential order. The reader can clearly understand the story problem and subsequent events. • The response presents descriptions and details that are moderately elaborated. • The response shows good control of language, although some errors in spelling, grammar, usage, and punctuation may occur.
2	• The response is a minimally successful attempt to tell a story in a logical way. It contains few elaborated descriptions or details, and may present a problem without resolving it. • The response is not consistently organized, and may be repetitive or lack a clear sequence of events. • The response shows limited control of language, and may include awkward constructions or errors in spelling, grammar, usage, and punctuation that make the writing slightly confusing.
1	• The response does not attempt to tell a story in a logical way, or it begins to do so but then drifts to other purposes or topics. It presents very few specific descriptions or details, and it does not elaborate on them. • The response causes the reader confusion because it contains incomplete or illogical thoughts, or does not show the order of events or how they are connected. • The response shows a lack of control of language, with errors in spelling, grammar, usage, or punctuation that make the writing difficult to understand.

Additional Comments: _____

_____

_____

Harcourt Brace School Publishers

Student _____ Date _____

Evaluator _____

Rubric for Persuasive Writing

The score of this composition is _____.

The composition has all or most of the characteristics listed in the chart below.

Score	Description
4 (high)	• The response is consistent and organized, giving the reader a sense of order and completeness. It presents an opinion in a logical way and provides well-elaborated, convincing reasons that support the opinion. Any minor organizational problems are offset by the overall quality of the response. • The response includes clear, relevant, well-explained ideas and opinions. It contains a variety of sentence constructions and vivid words and phrases. • The response shows excellent control of language. Most conventions of spelling, grammar, usage, and punctuation are followed.
3	• The response is a good attempt to present an opinion and support it in a logical way. The reader can clearly understand what the writer is trying to communicate. • The response presents reasons that are moderately or somewhat elaborated. • The response shows good control of language, although some errors in spelling, grammar, usage, and punctuation may occur.
2	• The response is a minimally successful attempt to present an opinion and support it in a logical way. It contains few relevant and convincing reasons and only minimally elaborates on them. • The response is not consistently organized, and may be repetitive or lack a clear order. • The response shows limited control of language, and may include awkward constructions or errors in spelling, grammar, usage, and punctuation that make the writing slightly confusing.
1	• The response does not attempt to present an opinion and support it in a logical way, or it begins to do so but then drifts to other purposes or topics. It presents very few specific reasons, and it does not elaborate on those reasons. • The response causes the reader confusion because it contains incomplete or illogical thoughts or does not show how ideas are connected. • The response shows a lack of control of language, with errors in spelling, grammar, usage, or punctuation that make the writing difficult to understand.

Additional Comments: _____

_____

_____

Student _____ Date _____

Evaluator _____

Rubric for Informative Writing

The score of this composition is _____.
The composition has all or most of the characteristics listed in the chart below.

Score	Description
4 (high)	• The response is consistent and organized, giving the reader a sense of order and completeness. It gives information in a logical way about ideas, people, places, steps, things, or events. Any minor organizational problems are offset by the overall quality of the response. • The response includes clear, relevant, well-explained ideas and rich, elaborated details. It contains a variety of sentence constructions and vivid words and phrases. • The response shows excellent control of language. Most conventions of spelling, grammar, usage, and punctuation are followed.
3	• The response is a good attempt to give information in a logical way about ideas, people, places, steps, things, or events. The reader can clearly understand what the writer is trying to communicate. • The response presents ideas that are moderately or somewhat elaborated. • The response shows good control of language, although some errors in spelling, grammar, usage, and punctuation may occur.
2	• The response is a minimally successful attempt to give information in a logical way about ideas, people, places, steps, things, or events. It presents few elaborated ideas, or it presents only one side of an issue. • The response is not consistently organized, and may be repetitive or lack a clear order. • The response shows limited control of language, and may include awkward constructions or errors in spelling, grammar, usage, and punctuation that make the writing slightly confusing.
1	• The response does not attempt to give information in a logical way about ideas, people, places, steps, things, or events, or it begins to do so but then drifts to other purposes or topics. It presents very few specific ideas, and it does not elaborate on those ideas. • The response causes the reader confusion because it contains incomplete or illogical thoughts or does not show how ideas are connected. • The response shows a lack of control of language, with errors in spelling, grammar, usage, or punctuation that make the writing difficult to understand.

Additional Comments: _____

_____

_____

Harcourt Brace School Publishers

Student _____ Date _____

Evaluator _____

Rubric for Descriptive Writing

The score of this composition is _____.

The composition has all or most of the characteristics listed in the chart below.

Score	Description
4 (high)	• The response is consistent and organized, giving the reader a sense of order and completeness. It presents a description of people, places, things, or events in a logical way. Any minor organizational problems are offset by the overall quality of the response. • The response includes a clear topic sentence identifying what is being described, along with rich, elaborated details that appeal to the senses. It contains a variety of sentence constructions and vivid words and phrases. • The response shows excellent control of language. Most conventions of spelling, grammar, usage, and punctuation are followed.
3	• The response is a good attempt to present a description of people, places, things, or events in a logical way. The reader can clearly understand what the writer is trying to communicate. • The response includes a topic sentence along with details that appeal to the senses and are somewhat elaborated. • The response shows good control of language, although some errors in spelling, grammar, usage, and punctuation may occur.
2	• The response is a minimally successful attempt to present a description of people, places, things, or events in a logical way. • The response includes a topic sentence, but is not consistently organized, and may be repetitive. It contains few elaborated details. • The response shows limited control of language, and may include awkward constructions or errors in spelling, grammar, usage, and punctuation that make the writing slightly confusing.
1	• The response does not attempt to present a description of people, places, things, or events, or it begins to do so but then drifts to other purposes or topics. • The response lacks a topic sentence and causes the reader confusion because it contains incomplete or illogical thoughts or does not include details. • The response shows a lack of control of language, with errors in spelling, grammar, usage, or punctuation that make the writing difficult to understand.

Additional Comments: _____

_____

_____

Student _____ Date _____

Evaluator _____

Rubric for Everyday Writing

The score of this composition is _____.

The composition has all or most of the characteristics listed in the chart below.

Score	Description
4 (high)	• The response is consistent and organized, giving the reader a sense of order and completeness. It expresses feelings or gives information in a logical way about ideas, people, things, or events. Any minor organizational problems are offset by the overall quality of the response. • The response includes clear, relevant, well-explained opinions or ideas and rich, elaborated details. It contains a variety of sentence constructions and vivid words and phrases. Letters include a heading, greeting, body, closing, and signature. • The response shows excellent control of language. Most conventions of spelling, grammar, usage, and punctuation are followed.
3	• The response is a good attempt to express feelings or give information about a topic in a logical way. The reader can clearly understand what the writer is trying to communicate. • The response presents opinions or ideas that are moderately elaborated. Letters include a heading, greeting, body, closing, and signature. • The response shows good control of language, although some errors in spelling, grammar, usage, and punctuation may occur.
2	• The response is a minimally successful attempt to express feelings or give information about a topic. It presents few elaborated opinions or ideas. • The response is not consistently organized, and may lack a clear order. Letters are missing one or more of the five parts: heading, greeting, body, closing, signature. • The response shows limited control of language, and may include awkward constructions or errors in spelling, grammar, usage, and punctuation that make the writing slightly confusing.
1	• The response does not attempt to express feelings or give information in a logical way about a topic, or it begins to do so but then drifts to other purposes or topics. It presents very few opinions or ideas. • The response causes the reader confusion because it contains incomplete or illogical opinions, is not consistently organized, or does not show how ideas are connected. Letters do not reflect an understanding of correct letter form. • The response shows a lack of control of language, with errors in spelling, grammar, usage, or punctuation that make the writing difficult to understand.

Additional Comments: _____

_____

Harcourt Brace School Publishers

Student_____ Date _____

Self-Assessment Checklist

Expressive Writing

Read each question below, and answer it by checking one of the boxes on the right.

	Yes, I did this well.	No, I need to work on this.
Did you tell a story about the subject you were asked to tell about?		
Did your story have a clear beginning and ending?		
Is the story clear and complete?		
Did you give enough details?		
Did you tell the story events in correct order?		
Did you keep your purpose and audience in mind?		
Did you use a variety of sentence types?		
Did you use interesting words and phrases?		
Did you proofread to correct any mistakes in grammar or spelling?		

Did you share this piece of writing with someone else? _____ If so, how did that

person's comments help you? _____

_____

What do you like best about the story you wrote? _____

_____

_____

What would you do differently the next time your write a story? _____

_____

_____

_____

Student_____ Date _____

Self-Assessment Checklist
Persuasive Writing

Read each question below, and answer it by checking one of the boxes on the right.

	Yes, I did this well.	No, I need to work on this.
Did you present an opinion about a topic?		
Did you give reasons to support your opinion?		
Are your reasons clear, complete, and convincing?		
Did you give enough details or examples?		
Did you keep to the topic?		
Did you keep your purpose and audience in mind?		
Did you use a variety of sentence types?		
Did you use interesting words and phrases?		
Did you proofread to correct any mistakes in grammar or spelling?		

Did you share this piece of writing with someone else? _____ If so, how did that

person's comments help you? _____

_____

_____

Do you think you did a good job of supporting your opinion? Why or why not?

_____

_____

What can you do better in the future? _____

_____

_____

Harcourt Brace School Publishers

Student_____ Date _____

Self-Assessment Checklist
Informative Writing

Read each question below, and answer it by checking one of the boxes on the right.

	Yes, I did this well.	No, I need to work on this.
Did you give the information you were asked to give?		
Did you give the information in an organized way?		
Is the information clear and complete?		
Did you give enough details or examples?		
Did you keep to the topic?		
Did you keep your purpose and audience in mind?		
Did you use a variety of sentence types?		
Did you use interesting words and phrases?		
Did you proofread to correct any mistakes in grammar or spelling?		

Did you share this piece of writing with someone else? _____ If so, how did that

person's comments help you? _____

_____

What do you like best about this piece of writing? _____

_____

_____

What can you do better in the future? _____

_____

_____

Student_____ Date _____

Self-Assessment Checklist
Descriptive Writing

Read each question below, and answer it by checking one of the boxes on the right.

	Yes, I did this well.	No, I need to work on this.
Did you give the description you were asked to give?		
Did you give the description in an organized way?		
Is the description clear and complete?		
Did you give details that appeal to the senses?		
Did you include a topic sentence that tells what you are describing?		
Did you keep to the topic?		
Did you keep your purpose and audience in mind?		
Did you use a variety of sentence types?		
Did you use interesting words and phrases?		
Did you proofread to correct any mistakes in grammar or spelling?		

Did you share this piece of writing with someone else? _____ If so, how did that

person's comments help you? _____

_____

What do you like best about this piece of writing? _____

_____

_____

What can you do to make your descriptions better in the future? _____

_____

Harcourt Brace School Publishers

Self-Assessment Checklist

Everyday Writing

Read each question below, and answer it by checking one of the boxes on the right.

	Yes, I did this well.	No, I need to work on this.
Did you give information or express feelings about the topic?		
Did you present the information and feelings in an organized way?		
Is the information clear and complete?		
Did you keep to the topic?		
If you wrote a letter, did you include all of the five parts?		
Did you keep your purpose and audience in mind?		
Did you use a variety of sentence types?		
Did you use interesting words and phrases?		
Did you proofread to correct any mistakes in grammar or spelling?		

Did you share this piece of writing with someone else? _____ If so, how did that

person's comments help you? _____

_____

_____

What do you like best about this piece of writing? _____

_____

What can you do better in the future? _____

_____

Student's Name _____ Grade _____

Teacher's Name _____ Date _____

Perception

Essential Knowledge and Skills The student:	Not Observed	Emerging	Proficient	Notes
Recognizes that art develops and organizes ideas from the environment				
Understands that art can communicate ideas about feelings, self, family, school, and community				
Uses sensory knowledge and life experiences to understand artworks				
Identifies in artworks basic art elements such as color, texture, form, line, space, and value				
Understands the use of design principles such as emphasis, pattern, rhythm, balance, proportion, and unity				
Analyzes media, processes, and techniques in art				
Identifies moods, meanings, and themes in art				
Uses art vocabulary in discussions				

Creative Expression/Performance

Essential Knowledge and Skills The student:	Not Observed	Emerging	Proficient	Notes
Combines information from direct observation, experience, and imagination to express ideas about self, family, and community				
Compares relationships between design and everyday life				
Creates original artworks and explores photographic imagery using a variety of art materials and media appropriately				
Applies art elements (line, shape, color, space, value, texture, form) in artwork using a variety of art tools, materials, and techniques				
Applies design principles, or formal structure, (balance, movement, emphasis, pattern/ repetition, proportion, rhythm, unity, variety) in artwork using a variety of art tools, materials, and techniques				
Displays a variety of expressive qualities or moods, meanings, symbols, and themes in artworks				
Uses imagination, creative thinking, and problem-solving skills when creating original art				
Uses various media, techniques, tools, materials, and processes to communicate and express ideas, experiences, stories, feelings, and values				
Relates visual arts to theater, music, and dance				
Follows directions and art safety rules and procedures				

Harcourt Brace School Publishers

Student's Name _____ Grade _____

Teacher's Name _____ Date _____

Historical/Cultural Heritage

Essential Knowledge and Skills The student:	Not Observed	Emerging	Proficient	Notes
Compares artworks from several national periods, identifying similarities and differences				
Compares cultural themes honoring history and traditions in American and other artworks				
Identifies the use of art skills in a variety of jobs				
Recognizes art as a visual record of humankind				
Recognizes that media, tools, materials, and processes available to artists have changed through history				
Understands that art reflects values, beliefs, expressions, or experiences in a cultural context				
Identifies the characteristics of art from other cultures, and values the images, symbols, and themes distinguishing a specific culture				
Acknowledges and appreciates the artistic contributions of various groups in our culture				
Identifies and discusses artworks of a particular artist				
Recognizes various artistic styles				

Response/Evaluation

Essential Knowledge and Skills The student:	Not Observed	Emerging	Proficient	Notes
Analyzes personal artworks to interpret meaning				
Analyzes original artworks, portfolios, and exhibitions by peers and others to form conclusions about properties				
Views and responds meaningfully to original art and art reproductions				
Recognizes characteristics that make artworks similar and different				
Distinguishes characteristics of style in art				
Responds to evidence of skill and craftsmanship found in art				
Respects the differences in others' responses to and perceptions of art				
Understands the difference between judging a work and expressing a personal preference				
Uses art vocabulary appropriately in response and evaluation				

Harcourt Brace School Publishers

Student's Name _____ Grade _____

Teacher's Name _____ Date _____

Portfolio Checklist

Contents of my portfolio: _____

_____

_____

I chose these artworks because _____

_____

_____

Place a checkmark in the box when your portfolio is complete.

Things to check   **Notes**

☐   I have included all artwork required.

☐   My presentation is organized and neat.

☐   My artwork is imaginative and original.

☐   I have used different types of media and materials.

The types of artwork I would like to design next are _____

_____

_____

To make my artwork better next time I could _____

_____

_____

Revising and Proofreading Checklist

Revising

☐ Is my topic right for this writing form?

☐ Is my main idea clear?

☐ Have I used vivid and descriptive language?

☐ Have I included different types of sentences?

☐ Do all the detail sentences tell about my main idea?

☐ Are my details in the order that will make sense to my audience?

Proofreading

☐ Is each part of speech used correctly?

☐ Do the parts of each sentence agree?

☐ Do I have any run-on sentences or fragments?

☐ Are capital letters used correctly?

☐ Are punctuation marks used correctly?

☐ Is each word spelled correctly?

☐ Is my handwriting neat and readable?

Student's Name _____ Grade _____

Date _____

Teacher's Report on Production Activities

Type of artwork _____

_____

_____

Description of content _____

_____

_____

Strengths _____

_____

_____

Weaknesses _____

_____

_____

Suggestions for future improvement _____

_____

_____

Review of Portfolio Contents

KEY 1=Limited   2=Below expectation   3=Average   4=Above expectation   5=Outstanding

Assessment	1	2	3	4	5	Teacher's Comments
Shows good planning						
Creates artwork that meets the assignment requirements						
Exhibits a growing sense of art technique and terminology						
Is developing a personal artistic style						
Creates imaginative and original artwork						
Expresses clear ideas, feelings, or thoughts						
Combines varied types of media and materials to communicate ideas						
Produces two- and three-dimensional artwork						
Expresses pride in his/her finished products						
Demonstrates improved technical knowledge and skills						

What suggestions can I give this student for the next assignment?

	For This Review					Since Last Review		
Overall Assessment Summary	1	2	3	4	5	Improving	About the Same	Seems Poorer
Amount of artwork								
Attitude toward artwork								
Quality of artwork								

Name _____

Personal Inventory
Looking at Art

What are the most important things you look for in a work of art? _____

_____

_____

What type of art do you enjoy looking at most? _____

_____

_____

Who is your favorite artist? Why? _____

_____

_____

What work of art would you like to share with your family? Why? _____

_____

_____

What do you think makes someone a good artist? _____

_____

_____

Where do you see art in your everyday life? _____

_____

_____

Name _____

Personal Inventory
Creating Art

Before you begin, how do you decide what to create? _____

_____

What materials do you most enjoy using? _____

_____

Of all the artworks you have created, which is your favorite? Why? _____

_____

What new type of artwork would you like to try? _____

_____

What type of art would you like to learn to do better? _____

_____

Check all the art activities you like to do.

○ Drawing   ○ Painting   ○ Weaving   ○ Sculpture

○ Photography   ○ Constructing models   ○ Making jewelry

Check all the kinds of materials you like to use.

○ Watercolors   ○ Tempera paints   ○ Pencils   ○ Markers

○ Pastels   ○ Clay   ○ Fibers (for weaving)   ○ Wire

○ Other _____

Word Cards

Pages 113–142 contain Word Card blackline masters that can be used to help students learn and review important art vocabulary. Words and terms identified in the lesson assessments and unit reviews are arranged by unit. These are followed by other important vocabulary from the *Art Express Pupil Edition* Glossary and templates for blank cards your students can use to make their own word cards.

Here are some suggestions for using the Word Cards:

- Distribute the Word Cards for words that appear in a lesson assessment. Before the test, pairs of students can work together to review their understanding of the words on the cards.

- Use the Word Cards as a springboard to review unit concepts. You might have students choose a card and either find or create an example for the word on it.

- Provide Spanish-speaking students with the Spanish and English versions of the Word Cards for a unit. Have English-speaking students work with them, helping them locate in the *Pupil Edition* an example for the word and reinforcing the English pronunciation of the word.

- Have students add the art vocabulary words to existing Reading/Language Arts Word Banks. Students can then use these words in any writing they do.

- Ask students to sort the Word Cards into categories. Allow students to come up with their own categories for sorting the words, and then have them explain why they chose those categories.

- Use the Word Cards to label types of art on bulletin-board displays.

- Work with students to attach to the various *Art Prints* appropriate Word Cards that identify art concepts found in the prints.

petroglyphs *unit 1, lesson 1*	outline *unit 1, lesson 1*	landscapes *unit 1, lesson 2*
foreground *unit 1, lesson 2*	background *unit 1, lesson 2*	middle ground *unit 1, lesson 2*
proportion *unit 1, lesson 3*	point of view *unit 1, lesson 3*	organic *unit 1, lesson 4*
value *unit 1, lesson 4*	contrast *unit 1, lesson 4*	diorama *unit 1, lesson 5*

paisajes

unidad 1, lección 2

plano
intermedio

unidad 1, lección 2

orgánico

unidad 1, lección 4

diorama

unidad 1, lección 5

contorno

unidad 1, lección 1

fondo

unidad 1, lección 2

punto de vista

unidad 1, lección 3

contraste

unidad 1, lección 4

petroglifos

unidad1, lección 1

primer plano

unidad 1, lección 2

proporción

unidad 1, lección 3

valor

unidad 1, lección 4

Harcourt Brace School Publishers

still life

unit 1, lesson 6

center of interest

unit 1, lesson 6

portraits

unit 2, lesson 7

contour

unit 2, lesson 7

relief sculptures

unit 2, lesson 8

profile

unit 2, lesson 8

abstract

unit 2, lesson 9

monochromatic

unit 2, lesson 10

shades

unit 2, lesson 10

tints

unit 2, lesson 10

unity

unit 2, lesson 11

rhythm

unit 2, lesson 11

retratos

unidad 2, lección 7

perfil

unidad 2, lección 8

matices

unidad 2, lección 10

ritmo

unidad 2, lección 11

centro de interés

unidad 1, lección 6

esculturas
en relieve

unidad 2, lección 8

monocromático

unidad 2, lección 10

unidad

unidad 2, lección 11

bodegón

unidad 1, lección 6

contorno

unidad 2, lección 7

abstracto

unidad 2, lección 9

tintes

unidad 2, lección 10

sculptures

unit 3, lesson 13

cartoonist

unit 3, lesson 14

print

unit 3, lesson 16

realistic

unit 3, lesson 18

diagonal lines

unit 2, lesson 12

comic strip

unit 3, lesson 14

coats of arms

unit 3, lesson 15

style

unit 3, lesson 18

movement

unit 2, lesson 12

three-dimensional

unit 3, lesson 13

symbols

unit 3, lesson 15

cityscape

unit 3, lesson 17

esculturas

unidad 3, lección 13

caricaturista

unidad 3, lección 14

grabado

unidad 3, lección 16

realístico

unidad 3, lección 18

líneas diagonales

unidad 2, lección 12

tira cómica

unidad 3, lección 14

escudos
de armas

unidad 3, lección 15

estilo

unidad 3, lección 18

movimiento

unidad 2, lección 12

tridimensional

unidad 3, lección 13

símbolos

unidad 3, lección 15

vista de la
ciudad

unidad 3, lección 17

Harcourt Brace School Publishers

Harcourt Brace School Publishers

variety *unit 4, lesson 19*	actual *unit 4, lesson 20*	vessels *unit 4, lesson 21*	radial balance *unit 4, lesson 22*
stylized *unit 3, lesson 18*	negative shapes *unit 4, lesson 20*	pottery *unit 4, lesson 21*	kiln *unit 4, lesson 21*
impressionistic *unit 3, lesson 18*	positive shapes *unit 4, lesson 20*	implied *unit 4, lesson 20*	potter *unit 4, lesson 21*

| variedad

unidad 4, lección 19 | estilizado

unidad 3, lección 18 | impresionista

unidad 3, lección 18 |
|---|---|---|
| real

unidad 4, lección 20 | formas
negativas

unidad 4, lección 20 | formas positivas

unidad 4, lección 20 |
| vasijas

unidad 4, lección 21 | alfarería

unidad 4, lección 21 | implícito

unidad 4, lección 20 |
| equilibrio radial

unidad 4, lección 22 | horno

unidad 4, lección 21 | alfarero

unidad 4, lección 21 |

Harcourt Brace School Publishers

ornaments unit 4, lesson 22	**architecture** unit 4, lesson 23	**pyramid** unit 4, lesson 23
puppets unit 4, lesson 24	**marionette** unit 4, lesson 24	**shadow puppet** unit 4, lesson 24
photography unit 5, lesson 25	**worm's-eye** unit 5, lesson 25	**bird's-eye** unit 5, lesson 25
memorials unit 5, lesson 26	**maquette** unit 5, lesson 26	**mural** unit 5, lesson 27

pirámide unidad 4, lección 23	**títere de sombra** unidad 4, lección 24	**visto desde el cielo** unidad 5, lección 25	**mural** unidad 5, lección 27
arquitectura unidad 4, lección 23	**marioneta** unidad 4, lección 24	**visto desde el suelo** unidad 5, lección 25	**maqueta** unidad 5, lección 26
adornos unidad 4, lección 22	**títeres** unidad 4, lección 24	**fotografía** unidad 5, lección 25	**monumentos** unidad 5, lección 26

cathedral

unit 5, lesson 29

translucent

unit 5, lesson 30

mobiles

unit 6, lesson 33

asymmetrical balance

unit 5, lesson 28

stained-glass

unit 5, lesson 30

Surrealist

unit 6, lesson 31

illusion

unit 6, lesson 36

symmetrical balance

unit 5, lesson 28

mosque

unit 5, lesson 29

lead

unit 5, lesson 30

nonrepresentational

unit 6, lesson 34

catedral	equilibrio asimétrico	equilibrio simétrico
unidad 5, lección 29	unidad 5, lección 28	unidad 5, lección 28

traslúcido	vidrio de colores	mezquita
unidad 5, lección 30	unidad 5, lección 30	unidad 5, lección 29

móviles	surrealista	mina
unidad 6, lección 33	unidad 6, lección 31	unidad 5, lección 30

ilusión	no figurativo
unidad 6, lección 36	unidad 6, lección 34

Harcourt Brace School Publishers

cave paintings	balance	action lines
color	collage	ceremonial
curved line	cool colors	continuous line
emphasis	detail	depth

pinturas rupestres	color	línea curva	énfasis
equilibrio	collage	colores fríos	detalle
líneas de acción	de gala	línea continua	profundidad

mask	geometric	form
overlapping	origami	mood
photographer	pattern	papier mâché
scale	repetition	primary colors

máscara

traslapo

fotógrafo

escala

geométrico

origami

patrón

repetición

cuerpo

estado de ánimo

cartón piedra

colores
primarios

space

warm colors

shape

two-dimensional

secondary colors

texture

watercolor

espacio

colores cálidos

figura

bidimensional

colores
secundarios

textura

acuarela

Harcourt Brace School Publishers

GRADE 4 • ASSESSMENT PROGRAM • Word Cards

Harcourt Brace School Publishers